HISPANIC
NOTES & MONOGRAPHS

ESSAYS, STUDIES, AND BRIEF
BIOGRAPHIES ISSUED BY THE
HISPANIC SOCIETY OF AMERICA

ANTONIO MACHADO Y RUIZ
By Joaquín Sorolla y Bastida
The Hispanic Society of America

ANTONIO MACHADO

By ALICE JANE McVAN

Corresponding Member of The Hispanic Society of America

WITH TRANSLATIONS OF SELECTED POEMS

PRINTED BY ORDER OF THE TRUSTEES

THE HISPANIC SOCIETY OF AMERICA

NEW YORK · 1959

By the same author

TRYST [poems]   1953

In *Notes Hispanic* (1942-45)

The Alameda of the Osunas

Spanish Dwarfs

The Villafranca Family and a Portrait by Esteve

———————————

Acknowledgments

For the opportunity of consulting material in various libraries of Spain, particularly the Hemeroteca Nacional at Madrid, the author is most grateful, and for the privilege of meeting persons who had known Antonio Machado. There was poignancy and pleasure in visiting places haunted still by the shadow of Don Antonio's large frame, in walking over the Sorian plain that had known his shambling gait, and through the streets of Segovia where the poet was known to most of his townspeople only as a modest professor who taught in a local school, in visiting his homes and the cafés and casinos where Don Antonio spent tranquil hours sipping coffee, composing verses, and chatting with his friends. It brought the poet near to leaf through volumes that had known the touch of his hand, and it was a deeply felt privilege to say a prayer before a tomb both obscure and famous, in the little cemetery of Collioure in southern France.

Gratitude is expressed to the poet's brother, José Machado y Ruiz, who graciously granted permission for the publication of the poems herein included with their translations, and to Eugenio Florit for the privilege of reprinting his poem, *Collioure*.

The 1940 (Mexico City) edition of Antonio Machado's *Obras* has been used for the Spanish text. Of the English versions appearing here, four were included in *Translations from Hispanic poets*, issued by the Hispanic Society in 1938. Many of the translations have been generously contributed by the following members of the staff of the Society: Ruth Matilda Anderson, Helen Eldredge Fish, Alice Wilson Frothingham, Jean Rogers Longland, Florence Lewis May, Adelaide M. Meyer, Beatrice Gilman Proske, Elizabeth du Gué Trapier.

Antonio Machado y Ruiz

1875-1939

Roman numerals refer to poems in his *Obras* (México, 1940).

DESPITE the traditional revolt of each generation of creative spirits against its immediate predecessors, the influence of those writers who formed the group known as Spain's "Generation of '98" has not as yet, though sixty years have passed, been dispelled. The force of its vitality was to sweep through the land like a fresh gale, driving before it the dusty leaves of inertia and giving back to those Spaniards aware of world currents their hope, their self-belief, and that fierce pride without which the people of Spain would perish. The year 1898 saw the nation meet with disaster: the loss of the Spanish-American War, of her ships, the remnants of her colonial possessions, and, for a time, of her confidence. Even the ebullient Sevillians must have been momentarily disheartened; there had been a saying around town that the next year they were going to hold their spring *Feria* in New York.

In the Spanish custom, groups of young men gathered in city cafés for animated literary conversations—it was Unamuno who called the café and the public square the true popular university of Spain—or, too high strung for sedentary discussion, they walked the streets at all hours, exchanging ideas on literature of the past, present, and future, naturally looking upon themselves as modernists and seeing in themselves the hope of Spain. The strange thing was that so many among them were destined to win recognition and exert influence, often far beyond the Penin-

1

sula. They went abroad while young and receptive, bringing back with them a widened outlook that might embrace German philosophy, French poetry, or English theories on education and sports, following the pathway opened by Francisco Giner de los Ríos, the great teacher without whom there might have been no Generation of '98. These men, said Ricardo Baeza, "broke down the wall, and Europe sprang into view."[1]

Soon they were publishing poetry, philosophical essays, novels, plays, usually forced to pay the printer who undertook the work, profiting little when they did receive payment. With some justification, they have been accused of pessimism, but theirs was a pessimistic attitude toward the evils of the day with their faith in the future shining through. Rarely can there have been a generation of youths more given to searching their individual consciences and that of their country. Coming into manhood in a time of crisis and transition, buoyant with confidence and vigorously intellectual, inspired by men of principles, they were determined to make the new century far different from the one that had just ended, leaving Spain diminished in the eyes of the world.

Pío Baroja, ever the iconoclast, denied that there was such a thing as a Generation of '98, calling it an invention of Azorín, his close friend, and adding that if such a literary entity did indeed exist, he was not a member of it. The label may not have originated with Azorín, but it was popularized in an essay of his published in 1913—and Baroja was heard many years later using the phrase "We of '98". No one group in any café was composed of these now famous men, and no master-disciple relationship, making for a closely knit unity, prevailed. But by one of those historical miracles that do occur, at a time when the need was urgent, a literary renaissance sprang into being, alive, alight, and many-faceted. Dámaso Alonso has written of one aspect of it as a "great poetic movement as genuine and broad as Spain had not had since the Golden Age, a full tide of poetry,

2

initiated by Antonio Machado and Juan Ramón Jiménez and still not in decline in the present day."[2]

Antonio Machado y Ruiz was born in Sevilla on July 26th, 1875, less than a year after the birth of his brother Manuel, also to prove himself a gifted poet. Their father was Antonio Machado y Alvarez, a scholarly man who, abandoning a professorial career to open up the field of folklore to research in Spain, achieved international fame in his work. He, in turn, was the son of Cipriana Alvarez Durán, sister to the poet Agustín Durán, and of Antonio Machado y Núñez, an interesting and talented personage who became mayor of Sevilla and rector of the university in 1870. Antonio the poet described in prose an eventful day in Sevilla that he certainly did not recall, the time when dolphins, lost and lively wayfarers, came leaping up the Guadalquivir and the populace crowded the riverbanks to stare and exclaim. There his father-to-be saw for the first time Ana Ruiz Hernández, who became his wife. It was a treasured day in the family annals; Antonio said that he almost believed, or perhaps dreamed, that he remembered it, a line reminiscent of Bécquer. By the time Antonio was born, the Machados, paternal grandparents included, were living in the Palacio de las Dueñas, then as now belonging to the ducal Albas. Either it was at that time divided into apartments or the poet's father was acting as sort of administrator; memories and the Alba records are not clear on this point.

Antonio was eight when the family moved to Madrid. Dreamlike memories of Sevilla haunt his poems: an atmosphere of heat and brilliance, his father going from his desk out into the bright patio of the Alba mansion, dark cypress trees against white walls made whiter still by the dazzling light, the fountain with a lemon tree bending lazily over it, where he tried one day to gather up in his small hands the yellow fruit reflected in the pool.

The removal to the capital was undertaken by the family as a unit when the grandfather was appointed to a chair at

3

the University of Madrid. By then the folklorist was father of four sons; José, who was to become an artist, and Joaquín, who was to travel to the New World, had been born. Life must have seemed promising to him with his growing family, a pleasant home, opportunity to devote himself to the work he had chosen, and the quiet fame of a scholar that began to come to him with the appearance of the first volumes of his compilation, the *Biblioteca de las tradiciones populares españolas*. In the series, he reprinted Agustín Durán's edition of the *Romancero general*, and the boys' grandmother would often read to them from this work of her brother's. Antonio said that he learned to read from the *Romancero* "compiled by my good uncle", since he and Manuel, avid to enjoy their favorites again or to discover new delights, would struggle with the printed pages by day. Their father also read to them evenings, ranging from Bécquer's legends to translations of Dickens and Shakespeare. Possibly the boys' grandmother and father had more time for them than their mother, who must have been busy with the successive babies. By 1887 Señor Machado, who had been an only child himself, was writing to a friend that he was finding it difficult to raise six children on his income.

Antonio wrote two accounts of a childhood incident, practically alike except that in one story his mother was with him, in the other, his grandmother, as though the two formed a single figure in his memories. Juan Ramón Jiménez mentioned visiting their Madrid home in later years and seeing on the wall a picture of a juvenile Antonio, done by the even younger José, in which he was shown playing cards with his grandmother, perhaps the first of the numerous drawings and paintings of Antonio by his artist-brother.[3] Doña Cipriana herself had painted her grandson when he was about four years old. Having benefited from a careful education under her father's supervision, she had shared her brother's research and now contributed to her son's folkloric studies. Family relationships remained close, although inevitably there came times when the various

4

members could not be together. The two oldest boys, unlike in temperament, each regarded the other as his most intimate friend. They went about together, with José often making a third companion.

At the age of five, Antonio had entered the Colegio de Antonio Sánchez in Sevilla, but his real education began when he, along with Manuel, became a pupil at the coeducational school founded a few years earlier by Giner de los Ríos, the Institución Libre de Enseñanza in Madrid. The senior Antonio Machados were on friendly terms with members of the faculty, such men as Giner himself, Manuel Bartolomé Cossío who restored El Greco to his rightful place in Spanish art, Joaquín Costa, and Eduardo Benot. Twice the family moved in order to be nearer the school. At the Institución Libre, the brothers reveled in the freedom of thought, the energetic idealism, the interest in literature that prevailed under Giner. Antonio, especially, responded to the Castilian countryside, storing memories of long ambles with fellow students over barren land and through the rocky Guadarramas in the inspiring company of Giner. John Dos Passos wrote in 1922: "There is not a single outstanding figure in Spanish life to-day whose development was not largely influenced by this dark slender baldheaded old man with a white beard whose picture one finds on people's writing desks...and I rather think Machado is the pupil whose name will live the longest."[4]

All their lives Manuel and Antonio remembered the teacher with affection and gratitude. After his death in 1915, Antonio wrote a poem in which he pictured "the master" walking down a bright path, telling his pupils to mourn for him in work and hope, "a poem known to everyone by heart," said the English Hispanist, John B. Trend. Manuel, on the third anniversary of Giner's death, wrote a moving account of that sad day. The love for woods and fields, mountains and sky and crumbling old Castilian cities, the sympathy for hard-working, plain-living country people, the unchurchly—though never atheistic—attitude,

5

and a certain austerity that clung to Antonio Machado, derive from a combination of his own nature, family influence, and his formative years at the Institución Libre.

Having completed the courses at Giner's foundation, Antonio attended (1889-90) two secondary schools in Madrid, the Institutos de San Isidro and de Cardenal Cisneros. Thereafter his formal education was to lapse for a decade. The family fortunes were declining, although Manuel, the eldest son, remained in school. Both, drawn to literature and the theater, frequently spent mornings in the Biblioteca Nacional (whose first director had been Agustín Durán), saw as many plays as they could, and Antonio went often to the Museo del Prado.

Their friends made a lively circle and included "Ricardito" Calvo, son of one great actor, Rafael, nephew and namesake of another, and himself destined to become one of the luminaries of the Spanish stage. Sharing a liking for literature, they circulated among themselves a periodical in manuscript form called *La alabarda*, edited by the Machado brothers. One of their number, Antonio de Zayas, who later became the Duke of Amalfi, published a book of poems in 1892 and had a play performed in a Madrid salon. Ricardo Calvo looked back upon his youth in a recent interview, recalling how Zayas preempted the leading role while the others were assigned minor parts, and how Antonio Machado would have given anything at that period of his life to become an actor.[5] In another interview Calvo admitted that his own fondest hope had been to be a poet— "but I was with number one and being number two doesn't satisfy me."[6] The quartet of friends went on excursions together, played cards, had lively sessions of the Basque ball game called pelota, and were as far as possible inseparable. Zayas and Calvo were to remain the most intimate friends of the poet-brothers throughout their lives.

Manuel, having delved rather enthusiastically into the Bohemian side of Madrid, was packed off to Sevilla to finish his secondary education and then to matriculate in the uni-

6

versity where his grandfather had been rector and his father a professor. Hardly consistent with money-making proclivities is the strain of unworldly idealism evident in the males of the family, particularly in the grandfather, a doctor who gave up his medical career because he cared too deeply about patients whom he could not help; the father, relinquishing his university career for the uncertainties of a private research worker's life; and the third of these Antonios, the poet. The father left Spain for Puerto Rico where he obtained some sort of official position; illness forced a quick return. Too weak to travel on to Madrid, he died in Sevilla early in 1893 at the age of forty-five. The oldest of his children was not yet out of his teens. When the grandfather, mainstay of the home, died two years later, the large family was left in precarious circumstances. Antonio considered going to Guatemala as his grandfather and an uncle had done to their profit, but the family decision was that young Joaquín should go. It has been surmised that this remained a thorn in Antonio's conscience.

Among the men mourning the loss of the youth's grandfather and trying to comfort the family was Eduardo Benot. He and Francisco Pí y Margall (who had headed the short-lived republic established in 1873) were leaders of a group of older men accustomed to meeting in a café for discussions concerning political matters or, occasionally, poetry. Men of letters both, idealists and elder statesmen, they had long advocated the granting of complete autonomy to Cuba—nor can anyone say whether or how history might have been changed had they been heeded. Benot had been one of the brothers' teachers at the Institución Libre; he was to remain a firm friend. They were invited to attend his *tertulia* where, they themselves reported, they became rather tongue-tied, although other budding writers were often present. In the judgment of the older men, Federico de Balart was the great poet of the day; it would hardly have been courteous for the younger element to bring out the fact that Salvador Rueda was accorded that honor by the upcoming generation.

7

How and when Manuel found time to pursue his university career is a question. He must have been dashing back and forth between Sevilla and Madrid, for his life and Antonio's seem inextricably mingled still. His friends credited Manuel with the knack of somehow knowing exactly what sections of his books examinations were going to cover and of studying only those pages.

In 1895 Enrique Paradas founded *La caricatura*, first of the little magazines that were to spring up during the next few years, their pages open to novice writers as well as to those of reputation. The Machados lent their services to the fledgling periodical, contributing to it under pseudonyms and persuading men like Benot to write for it without recompense. As far as is known Antonio's first printed words came out in *La caricatura*, in prose (humorous articles, theatrical criticism, and satire) aside from some light verse. He had not yet chosen the path he was to follow. A year earlier Manuel and Paradas had issued a book of poetry with some *seguidillas* by Manuel dedicated to Balart and a few paragraphs written for the young authors by Rueda. The younger brother did nothing in haste; throughout his life he would ponder ideas, pictures, words, steep himself in a mood, let his thoughts run almost of their own accord into lines, stanzas, poems, and in due time they would appear in print, phrased with the author's own simplicity.

Had it not been for his brother, Antonio might have mingled less with the effervescent literary groups. It was in 1895, he said, that he met Valle-Inclán, new to Madrid but already startling in appearance, weaving legends about himself, and soon a vivid attraction in literary *tertulias*. The brothers knew Salvador Rueda and were seeing a great deal of their poet-friend Antonio de Zayas. Two of the Sawa brothers were among their acquaintances: Miguel, who reminded Baroja of "Tick" (the wily Mr. Tigg) in *Martin Chuzzlewit*, and Alejandro, friend of Verlaine and the great poet's companion at the end, friend as well of Rubén Darío. "The incorrigible Bohemian," wrote Manuel of Alejandro

Sawa, "just back from Paris, talking of Parnassianism and Symbolism and reciting Verlaine's poems for the first time in Madrid."[7] Enrique Paradas and Francisco Villaespesa were in their circle which was always more or less in a state of flux. The brothers needed such stimulation, for they spent almost all of one drab year, after Manuel's graduation in 1896, on Benot's *Diccionario de ideas afines y elementos de tecnología*, their concern being with verbs. One of their co-workers was Ramón Caballero who later compiled the volume of Spanish idioms that is still a standard work.

When the war broke out, the brothers were in Sevilla—Antonio, apparently, for the first time since the family had moved to Madrid. They were astounded at the brashness of the Sevillians, their certainty of a swift victory, phrased in Andaluz, to the effect that North America was like a huge vessel fashioned from clay while Spain was like a small one made of iron.

In a few months it was all over, a turning point had been marked, and the youthful intellectuals of the land rose as to a challenge. This was the essence of the generation of literary giants to become known as the '98s: candid admission of the faults of the past and present, a clear-eyed approach to life, reverence for history and past greatness (the old towns, the early poets) allied with confidence in the future of their country and the determination to work for it. In the background was a new element, their awareness of the world beyond the Pyrenees.

Predestined for literary careers as they were by inclination, endowment, and environment, the Machados were confronted with the immediate need of becoming self-supporting when the prospect of combining these two objectives in Paris presented itself. The publishing firm of Garnier Frères had developed a line of Spanish editions. By the turn of the century the need for translators seemed inexhaustible, due primarily to the amount of work on hand but —as the Machados discovered after they had established themselves in Paris—for less attractive reasons as well. The

9

pay was minute and the work monotonous, the more so for creative minds.

A sojourn in France was in the family tradition; Antonio said that his father, grandfather, and great-grandfather had "all crossed the frontier and loved the France of liberty and laicism."[8] It was in March of 1899 that Manuel went to Paris alone, made arrangements for their work, and found a place for them to stay, a hotel in the Latin Quarter where Verlaine had lived near the end of his life. The tenuous association with Verlaine's spirit was the sort of thing that dazzled Manuel. Those, of course, were the last sad days when the French poet had been wandering in alcoholic confusion from one squalid room to another.

Antonio arrived in June to find his brother already a familiar figure in Bohemian circles, sponsored by Enrique Gómez Carrillo, a fellow employee about their own age who knew everyone in the literary circles of Paris whom he deemed worth knowing. From Guatemala, half-French and half-Spanish by blood, Carrillo had headed for Paris when no more than a boy, following the advice of Rubén Darío who always believed that but for his intervention Carrillo would have made the "tragic error" of going to Madrid.

So few are the comments left by Machado concerning his external life, they have been quoted and requoted. When Gerardo Diego was preparing his *Poesía española; antología 1915-1931*, the poet supplied a few lines regarding his travels. Four statements sufficed for his first plunge into foreign atmosphere, beginning with "From Madrid to Paris at 24 years (1899). Paris was still the city of the Dreyfus affair in politics, of Symbolism in poetry, Impressionism in painting, fashionable skepticism in criticism." Dreyfus was to be pardoned in the autumn and the affair was to drag on for years. Picasso was not to reach Paris until after the Machados, and although Impressionism may not have been superseded, Post-Impressionism was taking over and, far up in the ranks of the vanguard, Matisse and others, with no inkling of the name by which they were to go down in history, were already working in the Fauve manner. At any rate, it was literature that mattered most to the young man from Madrid.

Pío Baroja was also in Paris for the first time, his arrival and departure coinciding almost exactly with Machado's, although the Basque, a devotee of Dickens, was going on to England and then to other countries. In his memoirs Baroja told of the day that he and the two brothers, after lunching together, went out into the streets deliberately and successfully looking for a riot between Dreyfus partisans and opponents. He described other meetings, and it is evident that Antonio aroused the liking and admiration of Baroja, not as a writer—as such he would have been all but unknown—but as a man.

The Basque writer complained that he seemed to meet only Spaniards and Latin Americans in the French capital, and the Machado brothers, though they had wider contacts, were frequently in the company of Spanish-speaking travelers. Gómez Carrillo wrote to Darío from Paris, with the disdain of a true expatriate, "Today I found myself in a café, surrounded by Gauchos," and then added more cheerfully that the company had also included "two Andalusians (Antonio and Manuel Machado), artists themselves, who send you admiring greetings through me."[9]

The rest of Antonio's comments on this Parisian interval are: "I knew personally Oscar Wilde and Jean Moréas. The great literary figure, the great consecrated one, was Anatole France." The Greek Moréas, having abandoned his multisyllabic name along with his country and taken Paris for his home town, was an exotic figure whose poetry and personality had inspired an extraordinary interest in Rubén Darío on his first visit to France a few years earlier. "I plunged excitedly into Symbolism and became the friend of Moreas. Friend of Moreas!"[10] wrote the Nicaraguan who burst upon the world of Spanish poetry like a sunrise. Jean Moréas was the man who suggested the term of Symbolism for the new poetic movement. It was Carrillo who introduced Darío and

11

Moréas, and it was through Carrillo that the Machados met Wilde, by then a defeated man, his arrogance gone, wandering about the city incognito but still a charming companion in the best English tradition. The embryonic poets spent hours listening to the flow of his talk.

They met Paul Fort, the young Symbolist, aflame with life and talent, who was later to be elected by his fellow-writers Prince of Poets, an honor they had accorded in turn to Verlaine, Mallarmé, and Léon Dierx before him. Fort and the "two Andalusians" had more than poetry in common. He, too, was enamored of the theater and in his extreme youth had founded a flourishing little Théâtre d'Art for which Gauguin, Bonnard, and others in that circle had painted scenery. He had staged Hugo's *Hernani* and this play the Machados, collaborating with Villaespesa, now translated into Spanish, although, with its Spanish background, it had been translated and performed in Madrid more than once without success. Their version was to go the rounds of theatrical producers and some twenty years were to pass before it would be produced. The brothers were interested enough in art to attend Parisian exhibitions, and it is possible that through young Fort they met some of the painters of the day.

They became acquainted with Ernest La Jeunesse, well known even then as a critic, and the poet Laurent Tailhade, translator of *Don Quijote*, an older man with a stormy career behind him, lacking one eye, due to a bomb, and the use of his right hand as the result of a duel with Maurice Barrès. Manuel, writing of his glittering days in Paris, said that "all our gold was in the silken tresses of Alice and Susan, of Sonia and Marcella...,"[11] but he was not speaking for his younger and more sedate brother.

So little did their work for the Garnier house interest the Machados that it remains vague just what they were doing. In the light of their previous experience with Benot, they may have labored on a dictionary as did Alejandro Sawa and Gómez Carrillo, or they may have produced translations. No book on which they worked has ever been named. It is difficult to imagine Antonio as being very active in the determinedly Bohemian circles of Paris in which Manuel moved with such verve. United as they were by bonds of brotherhood and poetry, in personality and temperament their differences were extreme. It has been observed that even if Ricardo Baroja had not been the brother of Pío, he would have been his intimate friend. Manuel and Antonio would more likely have been casual fellow-writers barring their close relationship. Manuel was more convivial, the gay one, restless, witty, dapper, and more than once he was taken for the younger of the two. Acquaintances would address him as "Manolo" yet call Machado minor "Don Antonio", and those who responded to one rarely did to the other.

In his word-portrait of himself (XCVII) Antonio wrote, "I am in the good sense of the word, good," a concise and truthful line. From the same poem come these lines: "I converse with the man who always goes with me— / he who talks alone hopes to speak to God one day—." A man of great simplicity, grave, kindly, sparing of speech (except with close friends and on rare occasions), he was careless all his life in the matter of dress to such a degree that few who described him omitted this detail, the antiquated hat and bedraggled tie, the wine or coffee spilled on a shapeless suit already stained, ashes falling on burn-scarred and rumpled lapels, pockets bulging with an assortment of unlikely objects. He took himself to task for liking wine ("the stairway to dreams") and food and feminine companionship, regretting the results of one of his mild vices, a tendency toward portliness. An air of sobriety, even sadness, clung to him, and his manner was hesitant, often absent-minded, so that he has been repeatedly spoken of as "melancholy and timid", and as often described by words that are borne out in his writings, "serene and noble". Alien to his reserved and gentle attitude toward life is the older brother's self-portrait in *El mal poema* (Madrid, 1909):

13

This is my face and this my soul: Read.
Eyes of boredom, thirsty lips; agreed.
The rest . . . Naught . . . Life . . . Things . . . Nothing mysterious.
Escapades, light-hearted loves . . . Nothing at all serious.
A bit of madness, something of poetry, too,
a drop of the wine of melancholy's brew.
Vices? All. Or none . . . Gambling is not of my choosing;
no joy I find in winning nor regret in losing.
I take, not to deny my own land of Sevilla,
half a dozen glasses of manzanilla.
Women—no Don Juan, that I should abhor!—
but one there is who loves me well and another whom I adore.

Antonio was moon-struck; a stroll on a moonlit night appealed to the melancholy and loneliness so often in his heart. Manuel wrote in this same *Retrato:*

A ray from the sun, a smile opportune,
are dearer to me than the languishing moon.

Still, the brother-poets were complementary and, in their separate ways, needed each other. In Paris, Manuel was working in a frenzy of creation, composing some of his best poems; Antonio was maintaining his characteristic deliberate pace—and longing for Spain. There were group discussions of trends and techniques, with Darío's name occurring frequently in worshipful tones, much reading aloud of newly wrought poems, and celebrations when one of the youths had a volume published.

Baroja laughed over Alejandro Sawa's tale of an occurrence on a Paris street where he and some of his compatriots were chatting. A young stranger approached, ostentatiously Iberian in flowing cape and wide-brimmed hat, clutching a guitar, who explained that he could not resist intruding, so pleased was he to hear his native tongue again. Upon being asked whether he had been away long, he replied, "No, I arrived yesterday."[12] Which must have been the way Antonio Machado felt before long, stimulated though he was by the poetic atmosphere. Less than four months after he left Madrid he was back, leaving Manuel to see the World Exposition, to meet Rubén Darío and Amado Nervo, and to find inspiration for the poems that were to bring him early fame. Obviously, Antonio had accumulated some savings inasmuch as he was able to sign up for courses at the University of Madrid. Breathing Spanish air again and remembering Paris—he was always a poet who saw life through dreams and memories—Machado studied and wrote poem after poem, a diligent apprentice in the art he was to practise from now until late in life.

In the early years of the twentieth century, literary periodicals—*Germinal*, *Electra*, *Juventud* (with Picasso as art director), *Helios*, *Renacimiento*, and many another—came out like apple blossoms, colorful, fresh and new, fragile and ephemeral, but radiant with promise. The pages were studded with names that are now part of Spanish literary history: Unamuno, Valle-Inclán and Baroja, and among the slightly younger group (whose birth dates were only a few months apart) Ramiro de Maeztu, the Machado brothers, and Martínez Ruiz, soon to become Azorín. Pérez de Ayala was there, and Juan Ramón Jiménez whose signature looks strange, for he had not yet taken to writing out his middle name. The magazines themselves have become collectors' prizes. *La vida literaria*, directed by Benavente, was the first to print Darío and Jiménez.

The periodical that brought honor upon itself by being first to publish Antonio Machado's poems took its name from *Electra*, an anti-Jesuit play by Pérez Galdós that now seems mild enough. In 1901 it was looked upon as a daring attack on bigotry and an opportunity to loosen the grip Echegaray had long maintained on the Spanish stage. On opening night there was an uproar in the theater and the next day bands of university students roamed the streets of Madrid, demonstrating. The movement spread; in Barcelona, Valencia, Valladolid, youth took up the cry of liberalism in the name of *Electra*. On February seventh it was reported in *El país*, a Madrid paper, that "Authorization has been conceded by the civil government for publication of the fortnightly review, *Electra*, which will appear in a few days. Pío Baroja will direct it and various young writers, most of them distinguished, will collaborate." Manuel was among the founders and Antonio's first two published poems—it is unlikely that any earlier works will turn up—appeared in the issue dated March 30th, 1901.

Thus early are revealed two of his preoccupations: the sound of water that flows, splashes, glides, leaps, and surges through his verse, and the image of secret galleries wherein the soul lingers. The poem to which he later gave the title of *La fuente* begins:

> From the mouth of a dragon there fell . . .
> the cold laughter
> of water dropping to the basin
> with a frivolous, erotic murmur.

And the opening lines of the other are:

> Always, when the soul emerges from
> the dark gallery of a troubled dream . . .

Antonio was more inclined to rework and republish his early compositions than to abandon them. Both of these were included in his 1903 *Soledades*, considerably revised, but in no later volumes; they are among what Dámaso Alonso calls Machado's "forgotten" poems.

Antonio, consistent in the desire to channel his intellectual vigor, his upsurge of youthful energy, into poetic fields, was hampered by lack of a profession or an income. In 1902 he managed to obtain through Gómez Carrillo the post of Vice-Consul for Guatemala in Paris. Manuel went along, in high spirits over the success of his first—and as it turned out, perhaps his best—book, *Alma* (1901). Both were in a fecund period, writing with a sort of glory around them. What was worthwhile for Antonio during that second stay he compressed into a single line: "In this year I met Rubén Darío in Paris." Met him, no doubt, dreaming over those endless glasses of absinthe, more a god than a man of flesh and blood to those under the spell of his poetry. "I, too, admired the author of *Prosas profanas*," Machado wrote later, "but I tried—and note, I do not boast of achievements but of purpose—to follow a very different road."[13]

In June the Machado brothers, a familiar sight in Parisian streets, became three. They were joined by Joaquín, on his way back to Madrid from the New World. Strangely musical names were on his tongue; he had been living at Costa Cuca, Guatemala, between Retalulen and Quetzaltenango. There he had been farming, hard work in the company of Indians whom he came to like and admire, and there he had fallen ill. Paris revived him somewhat. With his brothers and Calvo, he explored the town and found himself suffused with delight to be mistaken for Manuel by an astounding number of women. At that period Manuel was balancing hours of intense work with hours of gay living; he and Antonio had separate quarters. Antonio seems to have had an ambivalent attitude toward Joaquín, eyeing him with a mixture of envy—Antonio would have liked to have been the one to cross the ocean—and guilt, for the youth had left home at a tender age.

On the first of August Antonio and Joaquín departed for Madrid, where the poet would ready for publication the poems he had been working on since 1899. Manuel, as before, remained abroad, flushed now with success and as much at home in the heady Parisian atmosphere as in the Puerta del Sol.

From their boyhood the two firstborn had felt an affinity with the world of the theater, reading dramas, taking part in amateur performances, spending more than they could afford for tickets. Furthermore, they had those young friends who were on the fringes of the magic carpet, Ricardo Calvo and Antonio de Zayas. Around 1900 Antonio Machado had been, for a short time, a member of Fernando Díaz de Mendoza's theatrical company, an opportunity won through the intercession of Balart, a family friend. José recalls him earnestly practising gestures and facial expressions before a mirror, and wondering whether a study of anatomy would help him to express emotions with body movements. When he left the boards, Antonio's longest role had consisted of perhaps half a dozen words. His failure as an actor did not lessen his interest in the theater; it was to come to fruition a quarter of a century later.

Pérez Ferrero explains that Antonio Machado's *Soledades*, dated 1903, actually came off the press late in 1902 when the author was in Sevilla, having gone there as the guest of Valle-Inclán to see the opening of a play translated by the latter. Ricardo Calvo was playing in it, and Machado went on to Granada with the actor, returning to Madrid early in the new year to find that his volume was being well received in literary circles. It was dedicated "To my dear friends Antonio de Zayas and Ricardo Calvo."

The luminous simplicity of the writer flows through this early work. Here are the pensiveness, the ambivalent feeling for death—an evasive virgin to be courted, an inevitable fate awaiting us all—and the pity for ragged beggars, the delight in every aspect of nature, even a self-identification with nature: "and something of earth within our flesh feels/ the dampness of the garden like a caress" (XXVIII).

Exuberance bubbles through occasional poems. After all, these were the years that Antonio would look back upon in a later poem (CLXIX), recalling how he used to take the stairs three at a time. He was tasting life with zest (XLII):

> Life today has the rhythm
> of undulating
> waves and of trembling ripples
> flowing and overtaken.
>
> Life today is filled with the rhythm of rivers,
> the laughing sound
> of waters running through the green rushes
> and over reedy ground.

In the closing poem, now so well known, Machado knelt to Jorge Manrique who five centuries earlier had meditated on death with grief and a serene acceptance of it. "Among my poets/ Manrique has an altar," wrote Machado (LVIII).

Already he was speaking of love lost, the chance for happiness past, picturing himself as remaining outside life, looking on, roaming the quiet countryside companionless, conversing with a fountain, the night, a day in spring. April and fountains are everywhere. "I adored the symbol of water and stone," he said in *La fuente*. The version printed in *Helios* two years earlier had been milder; he did no more than admire the symbol then. The fusing of mood and nature is in *Soledades*, the blending that prompted Spaniards to ask, "But where does the scenery end and the poetry begin?" Little in the volume foretells the power bursting forth, sometimes with anger, that he was later to display, nor had he developed the symbols embodied in his more mature work. No rhetoric decorates his austere verse, or ever would.

There was a reason for the quiet simplicity of Machado's lines. His taste led him back to the old writers, back to Gonzalo de Berceo, born in the twelfth century and the first of Spain's poets to escape anonymity, author of the famous work with the haunting refrain of the watchman's cry, *"Eya velar."* Berceo was the man who said so long ago that he wanted to write in the accents of the people. "And success in this," he added thoughtfully, "merits, I believe, a glass of good wine." [14] Antonio would have agreed with that, too. Machado read the Archpriest Juan Ruiz, that Spanish Villon, and Sem Tob, both of the fourteenth century, and the Perogrullo of folklore who would have been Manrique's contemporary had he existed. Lope de Vega, for whom the adolescent poet had felt such liking, did not lose that admiration when Antonio reached maturity. "I would counsel the reading of Lope before Calderón," Machado wrote when he was limiting himself almost completely to prose and accrediting the fictitious Juan de Mairena with his sentiments, "because Calderón is an end, a magnificent end, the cathedral in Jesuit style of the baroque literary Spaniard. Lope is an open door to the countryside, to a field where there is much to be gleaned, many flowers for the plucking." [15]

Modern literature the poet scanned with a colder eye. He

19

was obviously familiar with the work of the Spanish-speaking poets in the other hemisphere, and he had met some of them in Spain and in France. He knew well the Spanish poets who preceded him, having studied them in school, read them, heard them discussed in Benot's *tertulia*. Espronceda he referred to as "a very great poet"; there is movement, rhythm, life in Espronceda's verses. Machado knew the work of the gifted Rosalía de Castro and had assimilated that of Campoamor. Very likely he had read the prosaic poems of Joaquín María Bartrina who displayed, a generation earlier, the same bluntness that occasionally gives one pause in Machado's work, and that troubled, ambivalent attitude towards God, with the heart, confident that He exists, attempting to silence the mind's doubt.

Antonio dipped into foreign literature, reading Shakespeare, for example, and, of course, Poe. In *Soledades* the Spaniard called one poem *Nevermore*. There seems to be a trace of Rainer Maria Rilke in Machado, or a trace of Antonio Machado in Rilke, more likely indicative of similarities between the two men rather than of any mutual influence. And something of Heinrich Heine is definitely in Machado's work.

The one poet whom he read with delight, admiration, perhaps love, was Bécquer, that singer of enchanting simplicity, of sparkling rhymes and infinite charm. Aside from the old masters, it was Gustavo Adolfo who influenced Machado most, and even so, Machado sings in a different key.

The title of the volume brings Góngora's *Soledades* to mind, and Antonio de Zayas, writing an article on the early poet for the initial number of *Helios*, took advantage of the occasion to mention his friend's book. "Bright, fresh, sunfilled but tear-stained" it was, according to him. Like Verlaine and Darío, Antonio Machado admired the work of Góngora, but the sixteenth-century poet and the man of the '98s had little in common. Osvaldo Crispo Acosta has suggested René Sully-Prudhomme's *Les solitudes* (1869) as a more likely source for the title.

Slight indeed are traces of the possibility that Antonio Machado might have written differently had he not gone to France, become familiar with her poetry, associated with some of her writers. In essence and form his poems are Spanish. He would have read Sully-Prudhomme, first winner of the Nobel Prize for Literature (1901). The French poet's striking use of the word *sanguinaire* (in *Les stalactites*) to describe a torch in a grotto reappears in a poem by Machado (LXIII), used in the same context. The two men shared certain likenesses of personality—the conscience searching, the tenderness, the philosophic bent, the sadness that flowed for them into limpid lines. Both preferred the simple flowers of the fields, old houses, old things. The last poem in *Les solitudes*, too, had been of death, "the final solitude".

It is not surprising that the Spaniard called La Fontaine the first poet of France, Victor Hugo the second, nor that he admired the intricate structure of classic French poetry, even though he was inclined to criticize the land, her people, her writers. In 1904 he wrote to Unamuno, "Nothing [is] more foolish than to think, as certain French poets may have, that mystery should be an aesthetic element—Mallarmé confirms this by censuring the Parnassians for clarity in form. Beauty is not in mystery but in the desire to penetrate it."[16] The last sentence, firmly stated and provocative, is typical of Machado's prose style. In a private statement entered in a notebook and published ten years after Machado's death, he made a sweeping pronouncement to the effect that after Rimbaud French poetry entered a period of disintegration. A distaste for Valéry and his "frigid intellectuality" led Machado in the late twenties to deplore the tendency of certain young Spanish poets (now secure in their fame) to allow themselves to be "contaminated" by Valéry. This intellectual approach of the Symbolists disturbed him most, as absurd a thing, he said, as sentimental geometry or emotional algebra, and here again he was pointing an accusing finger at Valéry who had written of "the algebra of poetry".

21

Antonio Machado certainly would have read the works of the French-Belgian poets, Georges Rodenbach, well liked in Spain, and Émile Verhaeren. The latter, a writer of rugged charm, had traveled through Spain and in 1899 published an account of his not too favorable impressions. This work was illustrated by his traveling companion, Darío de Rogoyos, who later became a member of the Madrid *tertulia* the Machados attended. Verhaeren was attracted by Henri Bergson's philosophic thought, and it was Bergson who later aroused such interest in Machado, through his lectures and books, as to inspire the Spaniard to attempt to change his conception of poetry. It is pleasant, if not too enlightening, to roam the paths that Machado may have trod, to wonder about what may be chance similarities—Verhaeren's lines in *La grande ivresse:*

> Do you hear it . . .
> the little stream upon the pebbles?
> It flows and runs and glides.

and Machado's:

> The water of the fountain
> glides, runs and dreams.
> (XCVI)

Paul Fort asked "Am I Bacchus or Pan?" while the question Antonio Machado asked was "Am I classic or romantic?" Albert Samain wrote of such Machadoesque things as an old town with blackened walls, beloved mountains against the blue sky. There is a possibility that Machado met him, for Samain was in Paris in 1899 and he was a friend of Paul Fort. He was, however, very ill.

Machado brought back to Spain the works of French poets and continued to buy them through the years. He heard the melodious verse of Paul Verlaine recited both in Madrid and in Paris and there came times when, out walking with friends, he would deliver in quiet tones poems by Baudelaire or Verlaine. It may be that he was trying consciously to resist the latter's influence, so seductive then in Spain. In 1904 he wrote a poem to Darío "...who has listened to/ the echoes of the evening and the violins/ of autumn in Verlaine" (CXLVII), and in an undated letter to Jiménez he said, "You have heard the violins that Verlaine heard."[17] Geoffrey Ribbans calls attention to a work in *Soledades* that could be interpreted as Machado's deliberate and not always successful refusal to heed that music.[18] Called *Otoño*, this is one of the poems omitted by the poet in later volumes.

> The lurid autumn carries
> no legends to my ear;
> the chant of wind-borne fronds,
> of leaves dead and sere,
> since I heed them not,
> I have yet to hear.
> I do not know the psalms
> of leaves no longer green,
> only the bitter earth
> with its bitter dream.

Nocturno, dedicated to Jiménez, also made its sole appearance in Machado's first book. It was prefaced with an imperfect quotation from Verlaine—but neither is the Spanish text in this volume free from misprints and misspellings. In a review of a new work by Villa Moreno, written in the twenties, Machado mentioned the debt owed the Symbolists. Verlaine's melody, he said, "was not the music of Mozart, which still held the clarity, grace, and joy of Leibnitz' world, all illuminated and clairvoyant, but the music of his time, Wagner's music, the sonorous poem of the total opacity of being; spelled out, it was the metaphysics of Schopenhauer."[19] (Plato, Bergson, and other philosophers also found their way into this review.) As for Verlaine's famous "De la musique avant toute chose," Machado said that it mattered little what the French poet thought he was saying here, it was actually tantamount to a reaction against the Parnassian line that tried to sing. "The line cannot sing, nor is it its office to do so,"[20] wrote Machado. Reading Antonio's verses, one might wonder about this statement.

There were other French poets who might have appealed to him: Francis Jammes, lover of animals, singer of fountains, the less gifted and more sentimental precursor of Jiménez; François Coppée; the distinguished Henri de Régnier; and Paul Claudel. Cansinos Assens described the *ambiance* of his own youth in Spain as "The verse of Francis Jammes or of Samain, the music of Schumann, the fragrance of violets."[21] But Machado was purely himself, Spanish throughout, and it would seem quite natural for so solitary a man to entitle his first book of poetry *Soledades*.

Antonio was to broaden his repertoire of meters and forms slightly as he continued writing, but he abandoned none of those used in his first book. The eleven-syllable line, frequently combined with the seven-syllable in the style of the old masters, was a favorite of his. He used the attractive octosyllabic line and the alexandrine, which in Spanish has fourteen syllables and is not too strict as to where stress and caesura fall. Of his other meters, the principal one is the line of six or twelve syllables. Rhyme and assonance—so indescribably musical in the Latin languages—he liked. Only one unrhymed composition was included in *Soledades*. English translations from the open-voweled, sonorous Spanish with its wealth of feminine rhymes and its abounding assonances can do little more, as a rule, than convey the mood and meaning of the original.

Despite his withdrawal from the nonessentials of life, the poet would have been encouraged to be accorded recognition. Months before the book came out, Villaespesa in *El alto bohemio* had dedicated the title poem to Antonio Machado. Reviews were favorable, and Miguel de Unamuno, who had aroused in the younger man an early and never-to-be-diminished admiration ("the gigantic, very Spanish Unamuno" Machado called him), published an open letter in *Helios* (August 1903), welcoming him to the world of Spanish literature. Unamuno did more than write to him; he visited the poet at his home, and in gratitude Machado wrote a poem that was printed in *Alma española* (February 21st,

1904). Each admired in the other what he felt to be lacking in himself. Machado wrote, "I will give you the glory of a poet/ you told me, in exchange for a single tear."

Helios, one of the most distinguished of the ephemeral reviews of those days, had come into being in April 1903. It was truly international; the names of De Quincey, Maeterlinck, Nietzsche, Shakespeare, Goethe, and Emerson appear in the first few numbers. There are articles on Afghan literature, Polish poetry, Neo-Turkish writing, and mention of items of interest in reviews from Holland, Japan, and Germany. Even the places where some of the Spanish contributions came from indicate a restless spirit. Antonio de Zayas sent an article from Stockholm where he was in consular service, and Jiménez' translations of Verlaine came from a sanitarium near Bordeaux (he was then nineteen), although by the time they were published he was established in a suite of rooms in a Madrid sanitarium. Manuel Machado's work was represented before his brother's, but Antonio was soon a frequent contributor. Some of his best verses came out in *Helios*, among them the poem beginning *Y era el demonio de mi sueño* (LXIII), a work of eight lines in which fascination is combined with terror, and its companion piece, opening with *Desde el umbral de un sueño me llamaron* (LXIV).

Rubén Darío came to Madrid, renewed his acquaintances, and wrote then his tribute to Antonio Machado—or possibly only the first draft. He ended with the oddly touching lines: "I pray to my gods for Antonio;/ may they watch over him always. Amen." Antonio placed it before his own poems in his 1907 *Soledades*, and near the end of his life, speaking of quite another matter, he wrote, "I pray to my gods—as Darío said..."

Cansinos Assens told of Sundays in the early years of the century when the Machado brothers and other writers would walk the long road to the sanitarium where Juan Ramón was living or gather in the Madrid home of Villaespesa, and he presents an attractive picture of Antonio among the chattering café groups "like a great silent light". "I remember Antonio Machado," he wrote, "the grave singer of *Soledades*, as he was in the freshest days of his youth and of mine; and I see him with that pensive air, with that slow, vague gesture that many, on seeing him today, will take for the mark of time...But that gesture of grave indifference... was also the youthful habit of the poet." [22]

One of the few group actions undertaken by the Generation of '98 and used to prove the existence of such an entity, took place about this time. A manifesto in opposition to a proposed homage for Echegaray was signed by those for whom the dramatist was a symbol of narrowness and bigotry. The paper was drawn up by Valle-Inclán in 1905 and among the signatures are the names of the Machado brothers. Yet no group activity, no contact, no similarity of background need be argued to establish the actuality of the great generation; the men's unity of outlook and their extraordinary and diverse literary talents suffice.

Life as both brothers wished to live it was a productive affair with their powers exercised. Confronted with reality, it was the younger of the two who in 1906 took a decisive and very likely difficult step, withdrawing from his friends to study, his aim a teaching position. Concentrating his efforts on what must have been a dreary routine for him, he passed the examinations and the next spring received an appointment *por oposiciones* as a teacher of French grammar in a secondary school in Soria. Lack of a university degree foreordained a minor post. In May 1907 he went up to Soria to make arrangements for the coming year, staying during the visit in a boarding house near the Instituto, and it was there that he took up lodgings in the fall.

About 135 miles northeast of Madrid, the town of Soria, old and quiet, lies on the high mesa of Old Castile (of the provincial capitals, only Avila is higher), with the Duero River tracing its course from the foothills of Mount Urbión along a rugged way and forming near the town its "curve of a crossbow arch". Urbión's great mass rises from outcroppings of barren rocks to over seven thousand feet; in the sierra are water-filled ravines, among them the Black, the Icy, and the Long Lagoons. Winter begins in October and may continue through June, so that during much of the year the town is whipped by icy gales that sweep down from the giant peaks. In clement seasons, though the starkness of the boulders is unchanged and the horizon rimmed by barren mountains, green grasses and a few wild flowers soften the landscape, nightingales sing, the river rolls by, swirling as it passes under the bridge, streams splash among the rocks, pine-scented breezes blow, and twilight is a long, slow delight. The open land is rose red or tawny yellow, and beyond the town with its white, tile-roofed houses, the huts are built of baked earth, and a rosy glow seems to hover over them—save when the frequent thunderclouds govern the lighting. Nearby is the site of Numantia, "Rome's nightmare" in Machado's phrase. A place of local renown is the chapel built over the caves where San Saturio lived, supposedly in Visigothic times.

Machado would have been pleased by the Becquerian associations in Soria. "By San Saturio!" swore Bécquer in one of the legends Señor Machado used to read to his sons, and he married a Sorian girl whose mother's second husband Machado now came to know. Don Antonio was probably aware of earlier associations; the house in which Bécquer had died had been half a block from the first Madrid home of the Machado family, and at Giner's school the pupils were taken to sites of interest within the city as well as out into the surrounding countryside.

In 1920 when Gerardo Diego went up to Soria to teach at the Instituto, he was appreciative of the fact that both Bécquer and Machado had preceded him. By then, partly due to Diego's own influence, stirrings of creative efforts and an awakening of interest in intellectual matters were evident. But for Professor Machado, the circumstances of his new environment required a bleak adjustment, used as he was to the stimulus of literary friends. He held himself aloof from

27

the bickerings of the faculty, was friendly to everyone, evaded most of the social gatherings, and said nothing of his poetry. Kindly toward his young charges, he took little notice of them individually, nor could he find much in the teaching of French grammar to arouse his interest. Interminable drilling was expected in the school and Professor Machado was perhaps amused to recall a classroom memory of his own that he had described (V): the monotonous drills on a rainy day, the teacher

> . . . an elderly man,
> ill clad, austere and dry,
> with a textbook in his hand.

Years later, when he had all but abandoned poetry, through the lips of a fictitious *alter ego* Machado outlined a sketch of himself in the classroom: gentle, ironic, and philosophical.

In December the owner of Don Antonio's boarding house left Soria, arranging for the lodgers (a professor, a doctor, a draftsman, and the poet) to board with his sister-in-law, Isabel Cuevas de Izquierdo, and her family. The husband was a retired *Guardia Civil*, and it was the oldest child of this couple, Leonor, who was to be the inspiration of some of Machado's most moving lines. The girl was then an attractive thirteen; according to family tradition Don Antonio fell in love immediately, spoke to her parents and, in response to their urging, agreed to wait (in the Spanish phrase, *respetarla*) for a year before addressing himself to Leonor.

The year 1907 saw the appearance of his second book, *Soledades, galerías, y otros poemas*, referred to by the author as no more than an extension of his first volume. He did retain twenty-nine poems, abandoning the rest forever, but they form less than a third of the new work. A number of the poems in this publication had been printed in periodicals; Machado presented his readers with a surprise when he said that if different versions of a poem by him appear, that in the periodical is the revised form.

A reading of the body of his work discloses the rarity of

the setting and subject of *El viajero*, the initial poem in the book and in his *Obras*. As a rule, a scene bounded by walls, ceiling, and floor is connected with boredom in Machado's work—unless he is looking out the window. Even here he notes the autumnal surroundings without and their reappearance in a mirror within the room. The family is portrayed in an intimate moment, puzzled and disturbed by Joaquín, home again after his long absence, a stranger, aged beyond his years, in poor health, and without the traditional fortune of an *Indiano*. Antonio, so close to Manuel, never chose his older brother as the subject of a poem; his father appears once in a tender sonnet written long after Señor Machado's death, of which an early version, left unpublished by the poet, has been found. There are only incidental mentions of Antonio's mother; he seems actually to have recalled looking out at the world from his mother's arms. Antonio was godfather to his brother Francisco's firstborn, a warm relationship in Latin countries and one that might have held more than the ordinary meaning for a childless man. No mention of the godchild is found in his work, nor does Francisco appear, youngest of the five sons who lived to maturity, called "brother and heir" by Antonio. Francisco had ambitions to become a poet and published a book or two. References to Cain in the work of both Manuel and Antonio are insisted upon by some as having been written with Joaquín in mind. Still, Antonio credited Genesis as his source for the figure of Cain in *La tierra de Alvargonzález*, a later poem, and he regards the Biblical character from disparate points of view, once (in a letter to Unamuno) calling him the first tiller of the land, again commending him in a short poem (CXXXVI-x):

> Envy of virtue it was
> that caused Cain to slay.
> Glory to Cain! It is vice
> that is most envied today.

A new depth can be sensed in this volume, as in the stark verses *En el entierro de un amigo* (IV) and in the brief

29

poem (four lines!) on life as an interval of waiting for death (XXXV). A brighter enchantment marks certain poems, among them that on the lemon tree reflected in the Sevillian pool (VII). *Orillas del Duero* (IX), among the most beloved of his poems, is here, reveling in Soria in the spring—a fresh impression—and ending with the breathless cry, "Beautiful land of Spain!" Is it on a note of cynicism, which would be rare for the poet, or (more likely) with genuine commiseration that he ends a poem composed of ten quatrains (XXXIX), the theme of which might be described as "Alas for this and alas for that"? It all sounds Machadoesque from the opening stanza:

> Alas for him who, thirsty,
> on seeing the water flow,
> says, "It cannot calm
> the thirsting that I know."

until the surprising end:

> Alas for our first love
> with its faith so soon undone,
> and alas, as well, for the lover
> of our beloved one.

Despite the poet's own statement that it was "My custom never to return to what is done or to read anything I have written, once it is in print,"[23] a considerable number of the 1903 poems were revised, though often slightly. Aside from editorial revisions, there are omissions and additions as well as changes in words, phrases, and lines.

It was vaguely realized in the town that Professor Machado (the title was and is given to the highest category of teachers at the Institutos) wrote poetry, for his verses were appearing in Sorian periodicals. He was granted a mild deference as a man who had lived not only in the Spanish capital but in the French as well. At the time, Manuel's reputation was wider, although among the youthful writers in Madrid were many who looked upon Antonio Machado and Juan Ramón Jiménez as giants.

Gradually town and countryside became things of wonder to Machado as he strolled, with only his thoughts as companions, through the town, rich in Romanesque monuments and in tree-shaded plazas, and over open land where "only the water is heard". His feeling for the land grew to encompass the four seasons, the farmers who toiled on their small holdings, the shepherds in the hills. Gradually, too, he found men who shared to some degree his own interests, who read Unamuno and, later on, joined with him to found a little periodical. The group became accustomed to meeting in the casino that was the social center of the town and it was there, Gerardo Diego relates, that one of the men reproached Machado for having been secretive. They had found out, the man said, quite impressed, that Antonio was the brother of Manuel Machado.[24]

There was in Soria (at least from time to time) a man conversant with contemporary literature and a writer of verses himself, Manuel Hilario Ayuso, who had been a schoolmate of Antonio's in Madrid. The two became reacquainted in this city on the high Castilian plain. Unconventional in his ways, noisily republican, out of sympathy with his conservative family and disinclined to spend much time in the town of his birth, Ayuso was hardly one to undertake the role of mentor to the townsfolk in matters of poetry, or to try to explain how highly he himself held Antonio Machado. When the latter agreed to write the prologue for Ayuso's *Helénicas*, published in 1914, he was still regarded by some, and not only in Soria, as the lesser of the brother-poets.

The routine was eased for the new professor by infrequent trips to Madrid, long journeys made in a third-class carriage, his luggage light, as the poet reiterates in a number of poems. When Professor Machado returned to Madrid for the summer he was still a familiar figure in the literary life of the capital. By then Soria had become forever a part of him, and his great poems on Old Castile were beginning to take form.

Returning to classroom and boarding house for his second year, the professor may have been buoyed up by hope of a

31

forthcoming change in his life. The daughter of the house, Leonor Izquierdo Cuevas, was growing up; in June she had celebrated her fourteenth birthday. What sort of girl was Leonor? She has been described as a blue-eyed *trigueña* (more brunette than blonde) of delicate beauty and ingenuous gravity. In the wedding pictures Leonor's curly hair seems black and thick, her skin very fair, and she herself, beside the slim and personable groom, of doll-like proportions—like Antonio's mother. One picture shows her smiling with an almost impish charm. It has been said that Leonor had no artistic education but had seen much of humanity, a strange characterization for an adolescent girl in a tradition-bound community. Had she a lively, inquiring mind, an eagerness to learn? Was she gentle and submissive? Gay, companionable? Did she content herself with housewifely arts or did she look outward toward the vast world? Her father reportedly had a violent temper; it may have stirred Antonio's sympathies when anger was directed at the girl.

There are no love poems to Leonor until they came pouring forth after Machado had lost her. The feelings of Gerald Brenan, the English writer who lived in Spain for years and found himself being regarded as matrimonial material, may give a clue to Antonio's: "If I were to have anyone, it must be a village girl pure and simple who would make up for what she lacked in schooling by being a symbol, a point of condensation for this untutored life in which—or so I sometimes thought—I wished to sink myself." [25]

Described as brief, the courtship must have begun late in the school year. Heliodoro Carpintero has recounted the traditional formalities: the petitioning for Leonor's hand by Professor Federico Zunón, a fellow boarder and friend, in the name of Antonio's mother; the announcing of the banns in July, and the ceremony on the thirtieth of the month in the Church of Santa María la Mayor, with Señora Ruiz de Machado and one of the groom's brothers, José, up from Madrid for the event. Manuel, entangled in another escapade, had fled the capital for Barcelona.

Among the wedding presents were two inedited manuscripts of Bécquer's, given to Don Antonio by the second husband of Bécquer's mother-in-law. Judging them unworthy of the poet he so admired, Antonio burned them, an act requiring courage and absolute faith in his own judgment. Machado would have liked to know intimately every corner of Spain. After the wedding he and Leonor visited Zaragoza, Pamplona, Irún, and only political disturbances in Barcelona with the resulting disruption of communication prevented their going to see Manuel. Most of their summer was spent in Fuenterrabia, hard by the Bay of Biscay, a town with traces of Moorish occupation, of the Middle Ages, and with more than traces of the Renaissance. Antonio would have taken his bride to see the castle, the tower, the dungeons, and would have called her attention to the old escutcheons carved in stone. They must have walked many a time through the historic city gate to wander hand in hand over the countryside, and have spent hours by the bay, with Leonor marveling at her first glimpse of the sea. Returning, the bridal pair stopped off in Madrid so that the new member of the family might meet the others, including by now the oldest son.

Back in Soria for the third year and living as a boarder-son-in-law (since Leonor was too young to make a home for him), Machado was soon working on the poems that were growing, strong and beautiful, from the barren steppes of Old Castile, destined to win for him something greater than fame—the love, almost the worship, of his countrymen. This creative fervor was to continue unabated for years, holding him still in its grip—although the tone of his writing altered —after he had left Soria and had only his memories. No experience was wasted in this fruitful season.

The phrases he used to describe the river, the Sorian land, the people, are quoted so eagerly that they are threatened with becoming clichés: the "crossbow arch" of the Duero River; the Sorian spring "like the dream of a blessing" and again when "April contains a thousand rains"; the peasant with eyes "sunken, suspicious, gleaming above the jutting bones". A certain amount of local resentment regarding such lines as the latter must have been aroused, for on the day after the poem had been published in a Sorian newspaper, an "improved" version of this strong and forthright work (XCIX) came out in another local paper, with changes made in almost every line by an indignant hand.

Machado's denunciation of the present (XCVIII) was without equivocation:

> Miserable Castilla, once high over friend and foe,
> in tatters wrapped, despises what she does not know.

He held the belief that his own generation would restore Spain to her historic greatness. He was to be almost forty before he admitted its failure, and then, unlike many, he transferred his still shining faith to younger men who

> ... will go right,
> to divine light receptive, transparent and awake,
> like the diamond, pure, like the diamond, bright.
>   (CXLIV)

It was in the autumn of 1910 that Machado set out with a group of friends to explore the headwaters of the Duero, a trip involving travel by mail coach, on foot, and on horseback, the undergoing of drenching rains and exhaustion, the mastery of Urbión's peak and the view on the way down of the Black Lagoon (tarn might be a better word) with its aura of mystery and tragedy. Out of the expedition was to come a long work, *La tierra de Alvargonzález*, unlike anything else in the *œuvre* of Machado and written, perhaps in two of the three versions in which it was printed, in Paris. In the winter of 1911 he and Leonor were there with plans for a prolonged stay to be climaxed by a trip to England.

A grant from the Junta de Ampliación de Estudios had made the trip possible. What poems Machado had ready as a nucleus for *Campos de Castilla* were in the hands of Gregorio Martínez Sierra, who had paid the author three hundred pesetas for the manuscript. With this sum, his profes-

34

sorial salary, and the assistance from the Junta, Leonor and Antonio were off to a cold but enchanting Paris. Uninterested, obviously, in re-establishing literary contacts, Machado plunged into courses in philosophy at the university, and on hearing Henri Bergson lecture with the charm and insight that were his, the Spaniard began to ponder on what he termed "poetry in time". Bergson's theories, especially his postulation of the existence of two kinds of time, the false and that of inner truth, had had an immediate impact on literature, nor was his influence confined to France. Man had known before that movement does not measure true time; the traveling of a hand over the face of a clock, the slant of the earth toward the sun, have little to do with time as it is experienced. Bergson made this an important tenet of his philosophy. Time as the center of experience was thereafter of great importance to Antonio Machado; it followed that poetry written "outside time" was valueless. "The true poet sings" he wrote, "time, time and I!"[26] Proust, related to Bergson by marriage, achieved to an incredible degree the ability to make the reader feel with his characters the endless expansion of a moment, and today's novelists, especially in France, are trying to make time a fourth dimension in their work. Machado strove to convey in his poetry a sense of the past contained in the present, the future born of both and destined to become the past so that all is continuance. Often his ideas defy translation as in this line, used repeatedly and presented once (CLXI-VIII) as a complete stanza in itself: *Hoy es siempre todavía*—Today is always "yet".

Through the eleven stanzas of his poem to Narciso Alonso Cortés (CXLIX) the inexorability of time is dwelt upon.

> Time enwraps the heart of man with subtle net
> as a grove of trees is wrapped in river haze.
> Look not: all things pass. There is no return: forget.
> And anguish fills the heart of man—for nothing stays.

"Time will lap and gnaw and grind and flaw and corrode,/

undermine the rampart, perforate the stone." But poetry does not age—"and may your noble verse grow younger every day."

Intuitive by nature, the poet was drawn to Bergson's concept of intuition, the interpreter between intellect and reality, able to understand spontaneously, its truths superior to those achieved through effort. "Intuition", then, became another of Antonio Machado's philosophic watchwords, the sidestepping of logic to walk a shortcut to the bright vision of truth.

The poet related a conversation with a German student during this stay in Paris, claiming that he, Machado, was "moved more by the desire to draw him out in order to learn something from him rather than to stir up polemics" when he told the student that if war should break out and the Germans lose, Bergsonism would be enthroned in their universities.[27] Heidegger he studied later "for what he had of Bergsonism". Years were to pass before Machado, writing under the name of the nonexistent Juan de Mairena, would claim that a 1907 poem of his own, whose author he did not name, could have an unmistakable Heideggerian interpretation. In his unobtrusive fashion, the poet was calling attention to the fact that his "Heideggerian" thoughts were his own and that they had been published before the German's ideas were in print.

To the end of his days Machado read widely in philosophy (Manuel said that there were more books of this class than of poetry in the library he left), and he undertook the study of Greek in hope of reading the ancient philosophers in their own tongue.

In the little room where the couple lodged, the poet worked on *La tierra de Alvargonzález* (CXIV), the strange poem that may have been composed first in prose. Placed in the locale that had haunted Antonio since his ascent of Mount Urbión, it tells a story of greed, envy, and murder ("the blood of Cain"). In traditional octosyllabic verses the tale is unrolled against a Sorian background with the seasons wheeling by: spring when cherry trees are whitening, nightingales singing, and the storks are teaching their babies to fly; summer with the wheat gleaming like rubies; autumn saddened as the birds depart and the cicadas fall silent; the bitterness of winter with its whirling snows. The tale opens with the gay wedding of a farmer who has prospered; years pass, three sons have been born, and envy of the youngest runs through the veins of the older brothers. Miguel, the last born, is only a lad when he departs for the New World, having received his heritance from his father.

Time passes and the older sons become impatient; enviously they eye their father's rich farm. Finding the kindly old man asleep beside a spring one day, they yield to temptation. The poem tells of their leaving a trail of blood as they carry the body up to the dark waters in the wilderness of Urbión and how

> where secrets are well kept
> in the bottomless lagoon,
> with a stone tied to his feet,
> they gave him to his tomb.

The farm became bewitched: crops failed, disease struck the animals. When Miguel returned, upright, handsome, and prosperous, he learned that his mother had also died, of grief. The older brothers sold him the poorest fields, yet only Miguel's land flourished. Out hunting one day, he heard a voice singing of a father who had no grave in the earth; the spring murmured to the older brothers that their father had once slept on its bank, and wherever they went a *copla* sung by someone unseen would reach their ears, for the people of the town had surmised the truth:

> The land of Alvargonzález
> of riches knows no dearth,
> and he who tilled the land
> sleeps not beneath the earth.

Mysterious happenings disturbed the guilty sons. A spade striking ground came out bloodstained; a furrow just plowed closed up again, and a white-haired man was seen by one of them working in the garden by moonlight. He repeated to his brother in awe, "And the garden was a miracle! The garden was a miracle!" In silent accord, the murderers set out on a cold gray afternoon of November, inevitably drawn to the Black Lagoon. The poet's description of the wild scenery through which they passed is vivid. Darkness fell; they encountered "night, fear, and water".

> A wolf emerged, his eyes
> shining like two coals.
> It was night, a night
> dank, dark, and closed.
>
> The forest screeched. The brothers
> longed to be returning.
> Behind them, in the woods,
> a hundred eyes were burning.

They had no intention of returning; at the lagoon they plunged into its depths, crying out to their father as they fell. "And the echo, 'Father!' resounded from rock to rock."

Everything about the work is strange, including its history. A prose version was printed in Rubén Darío's *Mundial magazine* (Paris) for January 1912, illustrated by Daniel Vázquez Díaz; in April of that year, the work appeared in verse form in *La lectura* (Madrid), and before its inclusion in *Campos de Castilla*, published early that summer, the ballad underwent further revision. Facts appear to conflict again with Machado's statement that versions in periodicals are authoritative.

The problem of which was composed first, the prose tale or the ballad as it appeared in *La lectura*, presented a challenge to literary historians. Helen F. Grant, first in the field with a reprint of the story and her own study of the various forms, concluded that order of composition corresponded with order of publication. Various studies have been published on the matter; one would like to be persuaded by Carlos Beceiro who argues, in a detailed study, that the poem in

La lectura was the source for the prose. It seems to him that Machado buried rhymes in the prose, relocating them or, at times, replacing them with synonyms. One could take a passage almost at random and see the possibility that it could have been so. At the father's wedding, the ballad relates,

> hubo gaitas, tamboriles,
> flauta, bandurria y vihuela,
> fuegos a la valenciana
> y danza a la aragonesa.

In the prose the corresponding passage reads, "Hubo vihuelas, rabeles, flautas y tamboriles, danza aragonesa y fuegos al uso valenciano."

The time element is an impediment to acceptance of this theory. Those four illustrations had to be executed and cuts prepared. Nothing in the "feel" of the story indicates derivation from a poem. The narrative framework is well constructed and well maintained. Machado and a fellow traveler (who has no place in the ballad), having met in a diligence, are now on horseback, riding toward Vinuesa through the desolate landscape that had impressed the poet on his expedition to Mount Urbión where, indeed, he is heading in this story. Unlike the townsman, Machado notes, a farmer has no use for conversation unless it concerns crops or crimes. "Whenever I deal with men of the land, I think of how much they know that we do not, and how little it matters to them what we do know," he wrote. Reminded of a murder committed in the region years before, the countryman expatiates. Blind men had sung of the deed; he himself had heard it as a boy from a shepherd.

Many attractive lines in the prose do not appear in the two versions of the poem. Only in the story does the father, as he lies beside the spring, give thanks to the Lord for the good that has befallen him, and only there does the dream begin with an evocation of what he calls the best days of his youth, when "From garden plants and grassy meadow a harmony of gold and crystal arose, as if the stars were singing on land before appearing scattered in the silent sky."

The dream turns dark, a golden door within his heart opens hurtfully (a favorite conception of Machado's). Presently, as in the poem, he dreams that his sons have come to murder him and, waking, finds the dream reality. Only in the prose is there mention of the knife that is plunged into his breast as the one that he had used to cut the brown bread for his family as they sat around the table, and of the ax that bit into his neck as the one passed on to him by his forefathers. And only here do we read of the murderers' return from the lagoon, with nature dramatically shrinking from them. Two wolves, frightened by their aspect, slip back into the woods; the river takes a new course so that they cross over dry land; ferns, trees, even rocks, turn aside as they pass, and the bubbling spring beside which their father slept falls silent at their approach.

In every version, Miguel returns from the New World a rich man—unlike Joaquín Machado. Only in the prose is he described as bearing traces of the fevers he had suffered abroad. Does this deletion sound as though Antonio thought it might draw attention to the three Machado brothers, unlike as they were to the Alvargonzález men? Perhaps some friend, having read the story, made such a comment. The tale in *Mundial magazine* mentions, almost in passing, the murder of Miguel by his brothers. It is an improvement to omit this undeveloped detail, as well as the brothers' efforts to place the blame for their strange visions on the liquor they had consumed.

The *coplas* add greatly to the atmosphere of the poem; their use is amplified in the second version. The detailed picture of the Alvargonzález home is lacking in the prose. Machado may have been in such a dwelling on his mountain-climbing expedition, although he states in the ballad that the interior could be seen through the open door. One change made in the definitive poem *(Campos de Castilla)* is so unexpected as to arouse speculation. Why does the crucifix on a wooden chest *(La lectura)* become a pair of rusty spurs? Another minor detail catches the interest: at some time during those intervening months inflation had set in, for the hundred sheep inherited by the brothers had grown to a thousand. It might be that Machado, town-bred as he was, discovered that it took more merino sheep to constitute wealth than he had imagined. In an incident added to the final version of the poem, the older sons go hunting their cattle, which affords Machado an opportunity to add a long description of the land.

Dr. Grant has written that, were it not for Pérez Ferrero's book, it would be easy to conclude that Don Antonio sent the manuscript of the story to Darío and the first version of the *romance* to *La lectura* before leaving Paris. This valuable biography, replete with fascinating details, was written during the lifetimes of Manuel and Antonio, after many personal interviews, although it was not published until after their deaths. According to the author, the *romance* was sent to Madrid from Paris; there is no mention of the story.

Proof may once have existed that Machado first wrote the Alvargonzález story in prose. Certain of his notebooks were lost shortly before his death; one that escaped has yielded proof that *Los complementarios...Recuerdos de sueño, fiebre y duermivela* (CLXXII), did derive from an earlier prose version.[28] Beceiro is quite right in stating that the versions of this work are not so closely related as are the different forms of *La tierra*. Aside from the fact that these works, the tale of murder on a Sorian farm and the hallucinatory *Recuerdos de sueño*, were cast in both prose and verse, they are, for Don Antonio, of extraordinary length, subject matter, and tone, standing apart from the corpus of his writing and from each other as well.

La tierra de Alvargonzález displeased a few critics. Luis Cernuda, who says that García Lorca constructed a dramatization of the poem of which a single performance was given (a film has also been made in the very locale of the action), has called the poem an outright failure.[29] Certain reviewers regarded it as the most important thing in *Campos de Castilla*, "of classic flavor", with "the patina of time", "the Great Divide in his work". Machado himself expressed the fear that his poem might be taken as something based on an old legend, whereas what he had tried to do was to write his own *romancero*, very possibly a desire he had entertained since his childhood.

In Paris lines flowed easily from his pen; he was contented, even happy and fulfilled. But once Leonor had seen the sights of Paris and window-shopped, what could the young girl from the provinces have done with herself in that little room while her husband was studying, attending lectures, reading Unamuno, and composing poetry? She may have been content to be there at his side, to be living for a time in a foreign land. Perhaps for Leonor Paris was an exotic word. At times Antonio would read his new compositions to his young wife.

Pérez Ferrero describes the sad ending of their stay. Leonor became ill; on the eve of Bastille Day she coughed up blood and her frantic husband searched in vain for a doctor in a nightmare of battling his way through streets crowded with celebrants. The next day she was taken to a hospital.

By mid-September they were back in Soria. The distraught husband cared for Leonor with tenderness, built her a small vehicle in which he would wheel her around on pleasant days, moved in the spring to a house with a small garden, to no avail. The only certain, though oblique reference to Leonor during her lifetime appears in a poem dated "Soria, 1912" and addressed to a centennial elm tree that, half decayed, damaged by lightning, worm eaten, neglected by nightingales and trespassed upon by ants and spiders, had valiantly spouted new leaves with the coming of spring. The poem ends with Machado's admission: "My heart, too, is hoping...for another miracle of spring" (CXV).

They were back in their lodgings when Leonor died. She had seen the newly published *Campos de Castilla* and had pressed the volume to her heart. "I felt adoration for her," Machado wrote to Unamuno, "But pity is greater than love. I would a thousand times rather have died than have seen

42

her die; I would have given a thousand lives for her."[30] Leonor's death took place on August 1st, 1912, when she was a few weeks past her seventeenth birthday. She was buried in the Espino, the cemetery on the hill, and on the tombstone were carved her name, the date of her death, and "To Leonor / Antonio". Since 1943 a younger sister of Leonor has shared the grave, a new stone has been carved, and the personal message from Antonio Machado is no longer there. The two girls and their brother, the middle child, born of vigorous, long-lived parents, all died of the same disease.

The widower was quick to leave Soria. It was almost as though he had turned his back on the past—he even left in Soria the portrait that his grandmother had painted of him when he was about four years old—and on life, when he accepted an appointment to the secondary school in Baeza, near Jaén and on the Guadalquivir. Not quite Andalusian, not quite Manchegan, the poet described the town. Important battles took place there in the days of the Reconquest; ruins of handsome buildings remain, its central plaza with the ancient arcade is considered one of the most interesting in Spain, and the handsome building where Professor Machado taught had once housed a university classed with that of Salamanca.

Any illusions the newcomer might have had concerning Baeza, any expectations, were quickly dispelled. Nobody there was burning a lamp through the nights, trying to write poetry or to express the ferment of his ideas in prose; nobody subscribed to or had even heard about the literary magazines and the newly published books that passed from hand to hand in Madrid. What few well-read persons there were ignored contemporary literature. Who, indeed, was Azorín—Baroja—Maeztu—or even Unamuno? With the capital too far away for the weekend visits that would have meant so much to him, Machado was not living even on the periphery of the life he had always known. Rilke was in Andalucía that winter; he and Machado, born in the same year and so alike in some ways, would have found much in common had they met—and for Antonio it might have been an electric charge.

In a letter of almost incredible length written to Unamuno in 1913 from these "spiritual wastelands", Don Antonio expressed his dismay. Scarcely thirty per cent of the population was literate, he said, and "There is just one book store where they sell post cards, prayer books, clerical and pornographic periodicals. This is the richest region in Jaén and the city is peopled by beggars and *señoritos* ruined by roulette...At base there is nothing...Furthermore, this is Spain more than the Ateneo of Madrid."[31] He touched on a variety of subjects: the power of the church, the increasing domination of women (yet in more than one poem he expressed sympathy for the "caged women" of southern Spain), Unamuno's recent writings, and it was in this letter that he voiced his grief at losing Leonor. There was no one in Baeza to whom he could talk of these things; he poured it all out to his respected and beloved Unamuno. The poet mentioned his self-acquired education: "I lived in Paris for four years and I did learn something, though not much, there. In six years of going the rounds of fifth-rate overgrown villages, I have learned infinitely more." By this he probably meant not only that he had seen more of Spain and her people, but that he had read, studied, and written with little to distract him.

Within a month of his arrival, Señora Ruiz de Machado came down from Madrid to take care of her bereaved and displaced son. They took a house on the Calle de la Cárcel; the name of the street was apt. In Pérez Ferrero's words, or perhaps in Machado's own, the poet's spirit, too, was in prison. How long his mother stayed in Baeza is not known; the poet's exile lasted for years and he lived much of that time in a bleak little hotel room.

One of his fellow teachers also served the town as apothecary and it was in the backroom of this man's shop, rather than in the casino, that men would gather for conversation, especially on cold nights when the "stupendous" stove would be burning brightly. Cristóbal Torres, an intelligent man of warm personality, became Machado's most intimate friend. The opening poem of Don Antonio's *Nuevas canciones* (1924) was to be dedicated to his memory (CLIII).

A long poem (CXXVIII) presents a picture of Professor Machado imprisoned in his hotel room on a day of boredom and rain, with the clock in the corner ticking away. He has momentarily lost faith in his talent, mentioning disconsolately that he had formerly been "apprentice to the nightingale". Unpleasant the weather may be, but from habit his eyes turn often to the window:

> Winter, the fire gleaming.
> Outside, a fine rain streaming,
> now in fog disguised,
> now raining and snowing besides.

Reminding himself how good the rain will be for the land, resolutely he welcomes it...but the day is endless.

> Tick tock, tick tock . . . I heard you before.
> Tick tock, tick tock . . . Forever the same,
> monotonous and a bore.

"But is your hour mine?" the poet asks, thinking, of course, of Bergson. And then Leonor is in his thoughts:

> (Tick tock, tick tock). . . It is past now.
> (Tick tock, tick tock). . . Gone the day
> when what I loved most
> death snatched away.

He puts into words "The bitterness of wishing and not being able to believe, believe, believe!" Don Antonio lived outside the church, as his father had done. A story is told of his great-uncle, José Alvarez Guerra, who on his deathbed refused to kiss the crucifix, asking that a small bust he owned of Voltaire be brought to him. That, he kissed.[32] While Don Antonio's heritage, training, and mind led him down one road, he cast wistful glances at the path running through green pastures and beside still waters. No one who ever

45

knew Machado doubted that he was truly a godly man.

The Baezan poem, like the Baezan day, goes on. Of the books on his desk, the poet mentions two, a new work by Unamuno, unnamed, and Bergson's *Essai sur les données immédiates de la conscience*, the title given in Spanish. When evening comes at last, the professor dons raincoat and hat, picks up his umbrella, and goes out into the downpour for an evening of desultory talk—with samples quoted. He listens to the men making conversation and notes their frequent "yawns of Solomon". The freedom with which Spaniards, tired or bored, would luxuriate in this habit rather horrified Machado. He had mentioned earlier "a universal yawn"; now he narrowed the field of observation to his own land, alarmed by the lethargy of mind that he believed it signified. Some surprisingly prosaic lines on the subject (CXXXVI-L and LIII) were retained by him in his collected works:

> That Spanish yawn of ours.
> Of hunger, sleepiness, boredom bred?
> "Doctor, would it be that my stomach is empty?"
> "More likely, it's your head."
>
> . . . .
>
> Now there is a Spaniard who wishes
> that life, real life, would dawn,
> somewhere between that dying Spain
> and that other Spain of the yawn.

While Manuel and Andalucía (which is not quite the same thing as saying Baeza) were happily compatible, Antonio felt himself in a foreign land, referring to the town in such terms as "this Moorish city" and "my Moorish corner". In a letter to Unamuno written December 31st, 1914, Antonio said: "I continue here in this outsized Moorish village with no hope of getting out of it; that is to say resigned but not satisfied. To get out of here I should have to intrigue, make approaches, beg, things incompatible with my pride or vanity, I don't know which. In competitions they leap over me, even those younger in the profession and, truly, not because of their youth but because they are doctors, licentiates, I don't know what all! As far as can be seen, I am nothing officially. This, in a certain way, consoles me."[33] Actually he was not in the least consoled, attempting half-heartedly and in vain through the years of his exile to be transferred to Salamanca, Cuenca, Alicante. That he gave his best to his pupils is indicated by the words of José Gallego-Díaz: "His class in French remains forever in my memory and in my adolescent heart with the beauty of one of those rare spectacles like the aurora borealis, seldom granted us by nature during a lifetime."[34] Don Antonio was, furthermore, a man to make himself suffer rather than others, a fact to which this quatrain (CXXXVI-xxiii) bears witness:

> Wonder not, sweet friends,
> that lines my forehead score.
> In peace I live with men
> and with myself at war.

The habit of taking daily walks continued, sometimes with Cristóbal Torres, another indefatigable walker, otherwise alone. A little older, a little heavier, he might trudge down to the bottom of Baeza's hill, stop in at the tavern for a rest and a glass of wine, and climb up again with the help of his stick, or he might set forth on an easier walk, the pleasant one past the old walls, where he would stop to rest a while on a stone known as The Mayor's Seat. He, the solitary poet, had come to know loneliness.

At least his poetic inspiration did not fail him. Now it was olive groves that he wrote of rather than the live oaks of Castile, and the mountains he named were Cazorla, Aznaitín, Mágina. Over and over he thought of Leonor, recalling her childlike voice, her small hand in his as they walked across the fields, and living again through the night that she died. He addressed a nostalgic poem (CXXVI) to José María Palacio whose wife was a first cousin of Leonor's and who,

47

as editor of *Tierra soriana*, had published some of Machado's poems. The widower inquired about the Sorian spring, dwelling on the loveliness that he remembered and ending with the request that his friend Palacio go up to the cemetery while the flowers were blossoming, to "the high Espino, where her country is."

Antonio Machado proved that he understood his own nature very well indeed when he wrote: "Land of Baeza/ I shall dream of you/ when I no longer see you" (CLIV-iv). But, in the grip of his muse though he was, he suffered from that fear that his talent was exhausted. Only yesterday, he repeated, he had been an apprentice of the nightingale; today he "can sing no more."

In a number of works composed during these years with Spain for their theme, Machado rose to rare heights. The companion pieces, *Del pasado efímero* (CXXXI) and *El mañana efímero* (CXXXV) were written in a stern mood, one of disappointment in his own generation coupled with the belief that the new one would lead Spain on to triumph —in a national, not a martial sense. *España, en paz* (CXLV) was composed in November 1914. Physically, Don Antonio may have been trapped in a rainy little town where nothing ever happened; his thoughts were free to roam:

> In my Moorish corner, while the water destined
> for the blessed crops beats on windowpanes,
> my thoughts are wandering to far, embattled Europe,
> the barbarous north, enveloped in autumnal rains.
>
> Where the Gauls, the English, and the Teutons fight,
> over cavalry, cannon, tanks, infantry, all,
> there in ancient Flanders, on a chilly eve,
> a veil of melancholy, gift of the rain, will fall.
>
> . . . .
>
> A Caesar has ordered out the troops of Germany
> against the miserly Frenchman, the sad Moscovite;
> he has dared to harass Britain's tawny lion.
> Half a planet in arms against Teutonic might.

48

And his own country at peace—which state the poet salutes provided it is an honorable peace. As to that, he was soon writing to Unamuno: "Manuel says...that our neutrality consists of knowing nothing, wanting nothing, understanding nothing."[35]

Among the poems he was working on were distilled drops of philosophy and brief verses on the amusing remarks made by Andalusian gypsies—another facet of philosophy. His Madrid companions were often in his thoughts; he composed eulogies to such friends as Ortega, Jiménez, Unamuno. The deeply felt, masterly written poem on the death of Giner de los Ríos was dated four days after the great teacher's death, and the next year Machado was writing as beautifully, though less personally, on the death of Rubén Darío.

Luis Cernuda, for whom Machado's poetry reaches its peak during his early period, sees great merit in the later prose writings, describing them as "the sharpest commentary of that time", superior even to the philosophical writings of Ortega, though unappreciated when they were published.[36] It was during the Baezan years that Antonio began his cult of Nothingness, apparently haunted by his own theory that the world, created from nothing is nothing. Heidegger's much more solid contribution on the matter could not have influenced Machado this early, as has been mentioned, since Heidegger's nihilistic theories had not been published as yet. An underlying affinity linked the early existentialist thinking of the Spanish poet and the theories of the German philosopher. Machado never met Heidegger; when he did read the latter's works it seems to have been through the medium of a Spanish manual.

Julián Izquierdo sees Don Antonio as open only to Unamuno's influence at this time. The latter was reading Kirkegaard then and probably Machado was also, as well as Plato, Hume, Hegel, and Kant, all of whom are mentioned in Antonio's Baezan writings. Certainly verse does not always prove a suitable vehicle for the poet's philosophy:

49

Man is by nature a beast paradoxical,
an animal absurd, in need of what is logical.
He made a world from nothing and, his work completed,
said, "Everything is nothing—now I'm in the secret."
(CXXXVI-xvi)

These lines, probably written in Soria, were printed in
La lectura for May 1909. Many years later Don Antonio
composed a quatrain (printed twice in his *Obras*) that began
and ended with: "God said, 'Let there be Nothing'...And lo,
Nothing was made."[37] Consistent in his nihilism, Machado
did not develop it; Sartre would do that decades later.

The poet tasted despair and found it bitter. What more
could a man know of despair than to write: "We trust/ that
there will be no truth/ in anything we know." These lines
appear three times in the 1940 Mexican edition (CXXXVI-
xxxi, pages 707 and 817). Charm is apt to desert Don Antonio when he lingers on the flaws in mankind:

Man is rich in hypocrisy alone.
In ten thousand disguises the trusting he fools.
With a double key he locks his own home
and for another's house devises burglar's tools.
(CXXXVI-xvii)

Such graceless lines as these were, perhaps, aberrations
induced by the depression into which the poet-philosopher
sank and from which he would rise again, but it is an indica-
tion of the depth of his feelings that he did not delete these
and other lines from his works.

It must have lightened his heart when the critics praised
Campos de Castilla, particularly when they singled out the
Alvargonzález poem. Ortega and Unamuno are only two
among a goodly number who were generous with tributes,
and Manuel wrote that his being the older brother was not
going to prevent him from saying that he considered Antonio the deepest, most powerful poet in Spain.[38] Jiménez
for his *Melancolía* and Machado for his *Campos de Castilla*
were suggested in the press for the Fastenrath Prize. Nothing came of it, but the proposal indicated growing fame, and

the reputations of the Machado brothers were widened by the inclusion of both in the first edition of *The Oxford book of Spanish verse* (1913).

Apparently Antonio never praised Manuel in print; he may not have thought it seemly. Included with some private notes he recorded is a list headed "For a Study of Spanish Literature" which reads in part:

> Pure lyricists: Bécquer. Juan R. Jiménez.
> Neo-Baroque: Rubén Darío.
> Modernism: Manuel Machado.
> Lyric impressionism: Manuel Machado.
> Intimacy: Antonio Machado[39]

It was in Baeza, where Professor Machado's life was not a full one, that he began the study of Greek and found his interest aroused by numismatics. Starting in 1915, he applied himself to a course of studies in philosophy, taking examinations during the summers at the University of Madrid. In the final examination, which was oral, young Dr. Ortega y Gasset was one of the three men who sat across from him at the examination table. According to information given to the Hispanic Society by Don Antonio, he became Dr. Machado in 1918; he never used the title.

During the summers and Christmas vacations the poet lived with José and his family (and Señora Ruiz de Machado), having a room set apart for him in their apartment in a quiet, attractive part of Madrid, only a block or two from the café where he and Manuel and, often, José, enjoyed their *tertulia.* "Pepe" in those years was teaching at the Instituto de Segunda Enseñanza that had been established at the Institución Libre. Manuel and Antonio found much to do together; Antonio was a concertgoer, a frequenter of the Prado museum, yet he found quiet hours for his composing when most of Madrid was asleep.

The first summer in the capital was climaxed by Machado's participation in a homage to Azorín for his book *Castilla.* In the company of Cossío, Ortega, and many another old friend, Antonio traveled from Madrid to attend the luncheon in a hotel in Aranjuez. Afterwards, during the literary program in the royal gardens—with a fountain splashing in the background—he read his poem to Azorín, *Desde mi rincón* (CXLIII). Machado could see clearly the immutable Castile, frozen in the past, that Azorín saw. "This today that looks back to yesterday; and this tomorrow/ that is to be born so old!" Machado wrote. But he had faith in the future; his peroration began, "Oh, listen, Azorín, Spain is yearning/ to burgeon, blossom, all Spain is beginning anew!"

Sparse indeed were the highlights of those Baezan years. There was an excursion to the headwaters of the Guadalquivir, arranged to honor Joaquín who had made the trip from Madrid for a visit with his brother. Less arduous and less exciting than the expedition to the Duero's source, it was still an adventure and again the men met with a violent storm.

When a group of students arrived in Baeza on a cultural tour in 1915, led by Professor Martín Domínguez Berrueta, member of a brilliant family, a follower of Giner's ideas, and an old friend of Don Antonio's, a program was hastily arranged at the casino. Professor Machado read his Alvargonzález *romance*—an excellent poem to read aloud—and received an ovation. One of the students took part in the program, a slight youth with black hair and olive skin who came from Andalucía, his name Federico García Lorca. A protégé of Manuel de Falla's, he played some of the master's compositions and then folk music of Spain. The audience was loath to have him stop. These two performers—the sixteen-year-old electric and volatile, Machado perhaps more expansive than usual and certainly quick with sympathetic response—had a brief talk during which the youth mentioned that he was as fond of poetry as of music. Federico might well have added drama and art to his enthusiasms. His first published work, a volume of prose, grew out of this expedition. Twenty-one years were to pass before Machado would write the poem of blood-chilling beauty on the subject of Lorca's death.

Of Don Antonio's Baezan years, 1917 may have been the most pleasant. *Páginas escogidas*, with its prologue and biographical note, was published, and the Residencia de Estudiantes, which evolved from the Institución Libre, issued the first edition of his *Poesías completas*. There was an interesting trip through southern Andalucía, made after the poet had gone down to Puerto de Santa María for the christening of his niece-goddaughter. Two years earlier he had been there for Francisco's wedding, writing wherever he was, as a poem dated Puerto de Santa María and Sanlúcar de Barrameda, 1915, proves. This and certain others published in the August 1916 issue of *La lectura* were excluded from Machado's books. The second trip south was a delight, marred only by his being denied entrance to the building in which he had been born—and which now bears a plaque in his honor.

It was very likely during the Christmas holidays at the end of 1917 that Sorolla painted Machado's portrait (frontispiece), commissioned by Archer M. Huntington and now in the collection of the Hispanic Society, for in January 1918 Manuel dropped in at Sorolla's studio to see it. Disappointed in a portrait of Alfonso XIII on view there, Manuel decided that for all Sorolla's talent, the artist lacked the psychological insight necessary for portraiture and left without having seen the painting of his brother.[40] Antonio is portrayed looking spruce in the invariable black suit, holding the inevitable cigar. The lips, outstanding feature of Machado's gentle face, are faithfully painted, the upper tight, the lower full. There is color in his cheeks, the hair is black, and the eyes, as Joaquín described them, are like jet. The expression here reveals pride and integrity, qualities that, when ingrained, might result in an effect of humility, a word often used in association with Antonio Machado. Rubén Darío was astute enough to write, "He has an immense, Neronian, Diogenian pride."[41]

Manuel Monterrey, a poet who might have been better known had he covered a wider range in his work, had he written fewer sonnets to historical figures of Extremadura, earned his living as a representative of a clock company. In Baeza on a periodic business trip, he was stunned to realize, from pictures he had seen, that the man presiding with such humor and gentleness over the main table in the hotel dining-room was Antonio Machado. Monterrey was a shy man; a year and several visits passed before he gathered his courage and sought out Don Antonio. They had a chat in the latter's cramped little room. Machado remarked that his visitor must be a poet himself to love poetry so, which Monterrey denied, feeling unworthy to call himself such in the presence of greatness. He recited Machado's poem, *Desde el umbral de un ensueño*, and admitted that he never traveled without certain volumes of poetry, among them the 1907 *Soledades*. Don Antonio, of course, replied that all were excellent choices except his own book. The salesman-poet looked forward to his next trip to Baeza, but by the time he arrived Professor Machado had been transferred at last.[42] He began teaching at Segovia in the fall of 1919.

Only a pleasant jaunt from the capital and interesting in its own right, Segovia is noted for two disparate architectural marvels. In the heart of the city the famed Roman aqueduct arches nobly against the sky, double-tiered as it crosses the valley and swings alongside the Instituto building, set back on spacious grounds, where Don Antonio taught. And on a height, profiled against blue, is the Alcázar, archetype of fairy tale illustrations, the very image that is in the mind's eye when one dreams of castles in Spain. From his room Don Antonio could hear the bells of the lovely cathedral and those of many of the city's churches. He knew them all by name. The Eresma River flows by the town, its ravine-like banks green with grasses and trees from which nightingales are heard, or it lies static, ice-covered in a silent and leafless landscape. As in Soria, Don Antonio kept watch then for the returning storks, his symbol of spring.

He lived on the top floor of a house on rather a steep street —Segovia is a hilly town—with his private entrance in the rear through an iron gate on the Calle de los Desamparados. The gateway is now sealed and the door to the house blocked up within and plastered over so that entry is possible only from the street on which the house fronts. Today the tiny room with the shuttered window is a shrine. Here is the oil stove that kept the poet warm, the narrow metal bed on which he slept, the small round table at which he worked. But on the wall hangs a portrait by Jesús Unturbe, and on the table are displayed a bust of Machado, carved in Segovia by Emiliano Barral from the granite of nearby Avila, and a ceramic plaque by Daniel Zuloaga with a poignant quotation from Machado:

> On whitewashed walls
> of the traveler's cell
> my shadow falls.
> (CLIX-ix)

Filling two shelves are books, supposedly exactly as he left them although one bears the statement that it had been presented to the Biblioteca Popular by Antonio Machado. Among them are the translation of Tagore done by Zenobia and Juan Ramón Jiménez, French books published during the twenties (Verlaine, Baudelaire, Verhaeren...), and volumes by Campoamor, Jiménez, and other Spanish poets. There are no works on philosophy, yet Machado was reading philosophy in Segovia, his interest still held by Heidegger. When the poet was in residence, books spilled everywhere—in staggering piles on the floor, almost hiding the furniture, even the bed—and overflowed into the dining room where he ate with the other lodgers.

It was an up-and-down hill walk from Desamparados to the school. By now Don Antonio needed the constant help of his cane and within a few years he was astonished, even wounded, to find that he was increasingly helpless without his glasses, the usual sad discoveries of middle age. Teaching interested him less and less. If childhood memories are trustworthy, the professor would open a textbook at random and the fact that it frequently fell open at the same page left him unperturbed. It was his custom to smoke in the school-room and there were times when drowsiness would over-come him as he sat at his desk, due, in all likelihood, less to the droning young voices than to his own nocturnal wanderings and composings. On the street he would reach into his pocket and pass out gumdrops to small children; in school he was extraordinarily gentle with his boys. At least occasionally he would address them with humor and an irony that escaped them, indulging in a little private amusement. His mild eccentricities were less mild; whereas once he had been merely shabby, his overcoat now was ragged, his shoes of a type never seen on anyone else. For cuff links he had long used bits of string.

In Soria, Machado had been both teacher and friend of Blas Taracena whose death a few years ago deprived Spain of one of her most distinguished archaeologists. Down in Baeza, Rafael Laínez Alcalá, recipient in 1934 of the national prize for literature, had been a favorite pupil. Two future poets were in Don Antonio's Segovian classes, Alfonso Moreno, who has published several volumes, including critical writings, and Dionisio Ridruejo. The latter began trying his hand at verses in his early teens and admits (in the prologue to his 1941 edition of Machado's works) the "highly patent influence" of his teacher. In a book whose very title is one Don Antonio might have chosen, *En la soledad del tiempo* (1944), Ridruejo writes of twilight, dreams and love, of nostalgia for Urbión, Soria, the Castilian mesa, and of how he once experienced a sensation that he had become a part of those mountains near Madrid called the Gredos. Mariano Grau, destined to be a writer, was not a pupil of Don Antonio's since the boy attended another Segovian school, but there was a period when he would knock on the professor's door late in the day, whereupon Don Antonio would join him for a walk. Once away from the city streets, the youth might read aloud from recent books by the '98s or Machado might recite French poetry.

Machado was not to become a link between the generation preceding him and that following. The eruption of historical events in the world that resulted everywhere in a flaunting of traditional values had its effect on literature. Don Antonio's poems suffered no eclipse; they were read, quoted, and loved in Spain and far afield, and today's writers —men like José Luis Cano, José Agustín Goytisolo, Blas de Otero, Ramón de Garciasol—have turned back to Machado with a renewed appreciation that is almost reverence.

Antonio Machado stands alone like a stalwart oak, essentially unchanging—budding, leafing, turning russet and gold, bearing snow and ice with grace, demonstrating a majesty and strength that set it apart. The names of two poets are frequently mentioned with Machado's, due less to any likeness than to the appeal they carry for the man of the streets as well as for the literati: Juan Ramón Jiménez, who might be likened to an aspen, reflecting a thousand lights, whispering a thousand melodies, and Federico García Lorca of the next generation. Lorca is in a category by himself, unless on some as yet unknown planet there is to be found a tree made all of quicksilver.

Segovia and nearby Madrid were almost too lively; Don Antonio's poetic production lapsed. There were weekends in the capital where he spent much time in the home of Manuel, married now to a Sevillian cousin who had been his childhood sweetheart. The brothers attended literary gatherings, lectures, musical events, the theater, and soon were discussing the possibility of collaborating as playwrights.

Around the hilly town Don Antonio was a public figure. He showed less reluctance to give a talk or a poetry reading, preferring still, however, to address groups of working men. Having heard, almost at the moment of his arrival, that an attempt was being made to establish an *Universidad Popular* in Segovia, with free lectures and a free circulating library, the professor was prompt to attach himself to the movement. With his help, it proved successful and before long lectures were being given, at first in the normal school, then in a disused church. Books were made available, many

57

donated by Antonio Machado, the uncut pages having been ripped apart by his impatient fingers. The "University" still exists and the library as well, although access to the latter appears difficult, and the aims of the former may have diverged from the founders' ideas.

Don Antonio became a member of a *tertulia* that met either in a café or in the studio of the sculptor Emiliano Barral, which was in the chapel of an abandoned church, no longer in existence, up near the Alcázar. There were a dozen or more regular members and from time to time visitors from faraway countries would make an appearance. Blas Zambrano, another teacher (at the normal school), another tall man with a burly form and a ponderous walk and an absent-minded manner, became Don Antonio's companion. An irascible man and a terror in the classroom, Zambrano found his opposite in the equable Don Antonio. They shared humor and irony, chaffing each other and exchanging jokes.

Barral was a leading light in the circle, as was the ceramist Fernando Arranz who shared the studio and later became his brother-in-law. There were writers and would-be-writers, and a modest government employee who had memorized every poem that Machado had published. Two musicians were in the group, one of whom, Padre Villalba, sounds as though he ought to have been a man of extraordinary interest. His full name was Enrique Villalba Muñoz; he and three of his brothers were accomplished musicians, composers, and scholars, and all but one had joined the Augustinian order. A little younger than Machado, Padre Villalba had won praise from Pedrell for a composition written when he was nineteen; with his brother Luis he had edited the *Biblioteca sacro-musical*; he had helped with the founding of a branch of his order in Brazil. But in Segovia he was living in retirement and he may have been unfrocked; no one seemed to pay much attention to him. There was a piano in the studio; the group enjoyed music, conversation—and coffee and pastries.

At least comparatively, Don Antonio's days should have

JUAN RAMÓN JIMÉNEZ
By Joaquín Sorolla y Bastida
The Hispanic Society of America

JOSÉ MARTÍNEZ RUIZ   (AZORÍN)
By Joaquín Sorolla y Bastida
The Hispanic Society of America

been pleasant. But if proof were needed that this professor-poet was literally unable to live in and appreciate the present, it might lie in the story of his meeting with two friends from Baeza who had come north and were enjoying the sights of Segovia. Machado's eyes lit up when he met them by chance on the street and, as he extended his hand he said, "Baeza...Oh, that walk by the walls!" The little group was standing at that moment in the very shadow of the aqueduct.

Jean Cassou, the French Hispanist whose mother came from Cádiz, and who has said that there is no poetry he likes better than Antonio Machado's, went down to Segovia to meet the poet. When Don Antonio suggested climbing up to the Alcázar in the moonlight, up they went, the Spaniard doing the talking in his low voice and Cassou (in his own words) trailing respectfully behind. Unfortunately, the moon refused to shine. Cassou wrote of the Spaniard's work: "How to define its charm? What is it made of?...A tone, a note of his voice, a human accent, a sort of melancholy, harsh and sweet at the same time...the tone of a poor man who is also a great man—mysterious and silent."[43] He was quoting Darío's word-portrait here.

After Machado's death a few papers were found, and a notebook with ruled paper, the type that school children use, containing entries made by him in Baeza and Segovia. From references in the notebook it is certain that others once existed. Of minor interest are his notes on the literature of Spain's Golden Age, very likely an outline for class work. Having started teaching French grammar and literature, the professor had later been given Castilian literature as an additional subject. These perfunctory notes have been published in Bogotá.[44]

On the whole, the notebook, called *Los complementarios* by the poet, fascinates with its miscellany of thoughts, compositions, and personal items. In 1949 and later issues, *Cuadernos hispanoamericanos* included much of this material, together with studies by Luis Rosales, Luis Felipe Vivanco, Julián Marías, and other scholars. In the decade that has passed since, additional studies have been made by various writers, and Guillermo de Torre has published in one volume most of the contents of *Los complementarios* together with other inedited matter and scattered articles.

A cautionary word of Don Antonio's in this notebook would, if taken literally, halt any study of the man through his works, for he claimed that he was never so close to thinking a thing as when he had written the contrary. One learns that the still frequent excursions became less taxing physically as time went on, and that Machado, having been ill, found comfort in the realization that at any rate *"esta* too solid flesh" had been lightened. He may have come across this line later and chuckled over it; he used it in a 1921 letter to Unamuno. Many an entry reveals a private opinion, the summing-up of a book, a painting, a man.

There are poems in that small, meticulous script of his, including one about his having gone down by the Eresma River to read his Bible only to find that he had neglected to place his glasses in "their diminutive coffin" before leaving his room.

Interesting indeed is the early version (dated March 13th, 1916) of Machado's poem to his father.[45] He recalls his parent at a time when Antonio was seven and the father was out hunting on the banks of the Guadalquivir; then eight years later, in the garden of their Madrid home; and finally he pictures his father working, surrounded by books, shortly before his death. This early poem ends: "I am older now than you were then, father, when you kissed me/ yet in memory I am still the child whom you took by the hand./ Many years have passed without my thinking of you, father mine./ Where were you, oh, where were you in those years?" Once again he was trying to express time, inevitably moving on yet remaining static (in death, in memory). The published sonnet (CLXV-iv) ends:

> Your eyes have fled their morrow to yesterday
> and now are looking, father, down through time,
> compassion filled, because my head is gray.

Manuel said that his brother would often write a poem and later develop it in another form and meter. This freedom Antonio dared to display in translating one of Shakespeare's sonnets. Up to this time he himself had published only one sonnet, that to Valle-Inclán in *Campos de Castilla*. The notebook reveals that he was making a study of this poetical form; in it he copied poems by Dante, Ronsard, Camões, Góngora, and others, including Manuel. Of the two Shakespearean sonnets he copied, Machado translated one, casting it in a different form and writing airily below his work, "This is not exactly what Shakespeare says, but if the sonnet is read carefully, it will be seen that this is what he should have said."[46] The translation is given here as an interesting experiment on the part of the Spanish poet, in essence close to the original, in every other way radically different. Shakespeare wrote:

> When my love swears that she is made of truth,
> I do believe her, though I know she lies,
> That she might think me some untutor'd youth,
> Unlearned in the world's false subtleties.
> Thus vainly thinking that she thinks me young,
> Although she knows my days are past the best,
> Simply I credit her false-speaking tongue.
> On both sides thus is simple truth supprest.
>
> But wherefore says she not she is unjust?
> And wherefore say not I that I am old?
> O! love's best habit is in seeming trust,
> And age in love loves not to have years told.
> Therefore I lie with her, and she with me,
> And in our faults by lies we'd flatter'd be.

Antonio Machado rendered the lines thus:

> Mi amado, ¡cuánto te quiero!
> dijo mi amada, y mentía.
> También yo mentí: te creo.
>
> Te creo, dije, pensando:
> así me tendrá por niño
> ¡ella, que sabe mis años!

¿Es el amor artificio
de mentiras sin engaño?

¡Labios que mienten y besan!
Es tu mentira tan dulce . . .
Mintamos a boca llena.

It would have been a loss had Don Antonio's wishes regarding these informal writings been respected. He was explicit enough, writing that no one had the right to publish such notes; that he himself would never do so without revising them. The poet's admirers would have been denied insight into the man and his work. Here in his private papers is his account of the burning of the Bécquer manuscripts, his deeply felt prayer for Unamuno: "May the Lord go with him. May the Lord go with him. May the Lord go with him."[47] Here he named Virgil as his favorite poet, justifying his choice not by praising the *Eclogues*, the *Georgics*, the *Aeneid*—denying, rather, that these had influenced him and proclaiming the Roman's virtues as a man.

The compositions and notes in *Los complementarios* do not bulk large; their interest lies in the sidelights they give on the personality and mentality of Machado. He was occasionally mistaken as when, for instance, he wrote that if Jiménez were to continue writing in his "baroque" manner, he would alienate his public, a comment dated May 1st, 1917. In one respect it is a composition in this notebook, largely in prose, entitled *Fragmento de pesadilla* and dated Baeza, 1914, that may prove to be among the most valuable items in existence regarding Machado's method of composition, for it establishes the fact (mentioned earlier) that *Los complementarios...Recuerdos de sueño, fiebre y duermivela* (CLXXII), with its Dante-like background, germinated in prose. Whole sentences from the prose version, which has been edited,[48] reappear in the poetical version, out of sequence. The poem has been called surrealist and anti-surrealist. Gone is the sobriety of Machado's lines, the quietness —all is a swirl of feverish brightness, vividly imaginative, with scenes breaking off abruptly or wandering into other scenes as happens in a dream. A hint is given of a facet of the poet's life that has been practically unknown. "Mason, Mason!" voices cry out repeatedly through the fever and dreams. In a program for a Gran Festival Anual held in New York on October 26th, 1957, for Spanish-speaking Masons, Emilio González López published an article entitled *Antonio Machado y la Masonería* in which he states that Machado joined the Madrid chapter of the order and remained a member until his death.

It would never have been known, but for the discovery of the notebook, that Don Antonio had invented a whole school of nineteenth-century poets and another of philosophers, naming his creations, assigning them dates, and furnishing them with a little biographical background, sometimes even giving samples of their work. The imaginary Abraham Macabeo de la Torre, for instance, was a Jewish poet born in 1824 at Osuna who died at Toledo seventy years later and, according to his inventor, had been Cansinos Assens' teacher. Another poet, one Antonio Machado, born in Sevilla in 1895, had been a professor in Soria, Baeza, Segovia, and Teruel, and had died in Huesca, the exact date of that event being uncertain. "Some have confused him with the celebrated poet of the same name, author of *Soledades, Campos de Castilla, etc.*"[49]

The intention behind this pastime of creating poets, Machado wrote, was the making of a collection of nineteenth-century poetry without using the work of any authentic poet, and of doing a like sort of thing with philosophy. Among his philosophers, José Callejo y Nandin had as his subject "The Intelligence and Robinson's Island", while Eugenio March concentrated on "The Seven Forms of Objectivity". Fernando Pessoa, the Portuguese poet whose life span was a few years short of Machado's at both ends, also expressed his thoughts through imaginary poets, creating four of these who wrote in individual styles and carried on correspondence with one another.

Before long Machado's favorite imaginary poet, Juan de Mairena, himself invented a poet, one Jorge Meneses, and the latter in his turn devised a machine for writing poetry. "It is simpler than a typewriter," explained Meneses to Juan de Mairena, "A species of piano-phonograph, it has a keyboard divided into three sectors: the positive, the negative, and the hypothetical. Its phonograms are not letters but words."[50] By comparison, a typewriter would appear to be the essence of simplicity.

When the time came in which Don Antonio's writing was practically all in prose, he chose to speak through the best known characters among his apocryphal creatures, Abel Martín and Juan de Mairena, particularly the latter. Abel Martín, with the same initials as his creator, may have seemed too close. A curious exercise of the imagination, this; it appears that the poet felt the need of an intermediary between himself and his public when he descended to prose. It also appears evident that Machado wanted to reveal to his public aspects of his personality that found no expression in his poetry. Using these literary creations, he could view his professorial self with a detached air. "It is evident, my teacher used to say—and when my maestro said that a thing was evident, either he was not sure of what he was saying or he suspected that someone may have been positive of a contrary thesis..."[51] After all his years of teaching, the professor sounds surprised to find himself standing in a classroom making pontifical sounds.

In 1924 Machado brought out *Nuevas canciones*, his last volume of new poetry. Henceforth he would publish his previous work with additional compositions that might include poems of depth and magnificent lines though rarely would they introduce new themes. Repetition held no fears for Antonio Machado. Not only words but whole lines reappear, sometimes giving a unity to his work, again seeming a mannerism.

What he called "new songs" was material written, from more than internal evidence, almost in its entirety in Baeza.

As early as 1913 *La lectura* (Madrid) had published some of these poems. Among the few works undoubtedly of recent composition is the poem that Don Antonio read one spring evening at the famous Mesón del Segoviano, *En la fiesta de Grandmontagne* (CLXIV). The occasion was the honoring of Francisco Grandmontagne, the writer who had left Spain for Argentina some years earlier, carrying the dictionary, Machado said, that was his prayer book. In the same group was another exception, *En tren* (CLXIV), composed in 1923 and addressed "To the young poets who honored me with a visit in Segovia." In it is the often quoted line about Machado's knowing the route through the Guadarramas from Segovia to Madrid "rock by rock and branch by branch". Through the years the poet wrote a number of compositions on trains as he journeyed hither and yon in a third-class coach.

The opening poem (CLIII) in *Nuevas canciones* takes for its subject an olive tree standing half way between Ubeda and Baeza, pantheistically endowed by the writer with the intention of providing shade for a pensive man. His pensiveness leads him to Homer (the tree is worthy of being a temple for the gods), to Eleusis, Athena, giver of the olive tree, to Demeter and Persephone. There are many felicities here, as in the warm descriptive lines of harvest scenes: "big-boned and red, the oxen have come...and they hold the bountiful day in their eyes."

Following this comes a group of brief poems written in Andalucía and entitled *Tierra de olivar*, a heading changed in the collected works to *Apuntes* (CLIV). With only these for evidence, a tenuous silken thread could be detected linking Federico García Lorca to Antonio Machado. The impact of utter freshness in Lorca's poetry, his newly minted phrases, his oblique view of life, at once candid and poetical, seem to lift him out of the steady flow of Spanish literature. Perhaps no man can be quite that free from the world's continuity; in Lorca's early poems, and here and there in later works, Machado's influence seems to be traceable. More sur-

65

prising is the feeling that in Don Antonio's *Recuerdos de sueño, fiebre y duermivela* (CLXXII), written late in his career, the influence apparently flows in the opposite direction. The older writer admitted to great admiration for Lorca's work in an interview that took place during the summer of 1937. One would hardly expect a man of the '98s to say, as he did then, "It suffices me to read Jorge Manrique and Federico García Lorca."[52]

In this 1924 book the silken thread leading from Machado to Lorca often firms into a slender cord. There are the imaginative *Galerías* (CLVI), called *Apuntes para un estereoscopio lírico* in the book, and particularly *La luna, la sombra y el bufón* (CLVII), although the theme of this composition could never have been Federico's since he did not live long enough to find old age confronting him. There is a group of fifteen poems (CLIX), distillations of charm, patterned after Andalusian songs (the *copla*, the *seguidilla*, the *soleá*) and often reminiscent in sentiment and music of the German lieder, or in mood and delicacy of the Japanese haikai:

> By waters darkly flowing.
> Night over Málaga—
> sea foam and jasmine blowing.

Another poem, *Hacia tierra baja* (CLV, i-ii), is slight compared with Lorca's *Casa de Bernarda Alba*. Both works, however, germinated in sympathy for the restricted lives of Andalusian women. Machado notes a wistful girl sitting behind the *reja* of a Baezan window as he plods past on his way to a less than exhilarating evening at the apothecary shop. "I, too," he wants to tell her, "bear a lion within my breast."

Don Antonio included poems about Soria in *Nuevas canciones*, but it is a place remembered from southern Spain. He wrote of Leonor and the high Espino, painful memories. Among the most pleasing compositions are the stanzas telling of a summer night on the shore of Sanlúcar in the province of Andalucía, with this delightful insertion:

66

To a Japanese girl
said Sōkan quietly,
"The white moon above
I shall use to fan thee,
a white fan of moon
on the shores of the sea."
(CLV-iv)

Here is concrete evidence of the Spaniard's interest in Japanese poetry. Sōkan, born in the fifteenth century, wrote a well known haikai in which he saw the moon as a fan, with a branch, etched against the sky, forming the handle.

Some of the results of Machado's study of the sonnet are revealed in *Nuevas canciones*, classic in form although now and then he tried variants of the Petrarchian rhyme scheme (and never the Shakespearean couplet), foretelling occasional experiments of similar type. A number take fellow-writers for subject matter; there are sonnet-descriptions of Baroja, Azorín, Pérez de Ayala. That to Eugenio d'Ors is a post-Baezan work, dated 1921.

One composition (CLVIII-x), conveying the sense of wonder that the poet felt on seeing a rainbow by night, is dedicated to Ramón del Valle-Inclán, probably because he so liked exotic things. In the last lines Don Antonio was moved to beseech God:

And Thou, Lord, through whom we see,
who our hearts canst trace,
tell us if one day we
shall look upon Thy face.

Machado once said that for every noun, every adjective, there should be four verbs, as in Bécquer's writings. Nonetheless, it is when he is closest to following this canon, as in a number of brief poems in this book, that the appeal of his lines seems weakest. Too often is the tone dry and didactic in the group called *Proverbios y cantares* (CLXI), a heading used earlier for a similar collection. The *Revista de occidente* for September 1923 had published some of these, together with certain others omitted in the book, and some had appeared in *La lectura* in 1913 and 1914.

The first stanza expresses Machado's longing (felt by Berceo, too, long before) that men should try to understand the viewpoint of others:

> The eye you see do not construe
> an eye because you see it
> but because it sees you.

The second repeats the thought in another way:

> A conversationalist's mission:
> Ask first,
> then . . . listen.

Machado himself apparently became aware that his lines had taken on an admonitory tone, that they did not sound like a man looking inward, talking to himself (although hoping to be overheard), for he included among these verses one (L) with a conciliatory tone:

> The you in my song I deny
> alludes to you, my companion.
> The sense of that you is I.

More lighthearted are the verses in which Don Antonio quotes samples of the gypsies' unexpected remarks. One suggests to a friend that they stroll back and forth on the shortcut; another advises choosing the middle road—"You'll never arrive," he promises, and indeed the purpose of roaming gypsies is not necessarily to arrive.

The fifth proverb (or song) seems rather baldly put forth: "Between living and dreaming/ there is a third thing./ Guess what it is." Even though it rhymes in the original, it draws the reader up short. Some twenty pages later an echo is struck, a reply offered: "After living and dreaming/ comes what matters more:/ waking" (LIII). Nor is the subject dropped yet; a dozen pages farther on is found, "If it is good to live,/ it is better to dream,/ and best of all,/ mother, is to awaken" (LXXXI). Death, for Antonio Machado, was an awakening to something better than life.

Concluding the volume, he speaks of his poetic theories, advising poets that "The poor, verbal, temporal rhyme" is the rich one. The adjective and the noun, he says,

> are accidents of the verb
> that lyric grammar begets,
> of the Today that will be Tomorrow,
> of the Yesterday that is Yet.
>
> (CLXIV, p.346)

Critics varied in their reactions to *Nuevas canciones*, which can hardly be said of Don Antonio's earlier works. He had become sententious in tone, something new with him, wrote Roberto Bula Píriz. A review published in the *Revista de occidente* for June 1924 remarked on his indifference to the melodic line. But there were those who praised the pure lyric quality and "the rhetoric in which logic predominates". The poems found favor with the Andalusians, and Crispo Acosta, a man of discriminating taste, referred to the new poems as "bright, difficult verses". Over in Paris the International Society of Intellectuals awarded Machado a prize for his new publication. His next book would be the 1928 *Poesías completas* which includes sixty-odd pages of prose ascribed to Abel Martín and Juan de Mairena.

The year that saw *Nuevas canciones* published also saw the emergence of the Machado brothers as playwrights. Antonio had been working on plays in his Segovian room during the school week while Manuel labored in Madrid; on weekends they met to discuss, plan, and rewrite, setting the pattern for years to come. The day was to dawn when Professor Machado would be spending so much time in the capital that he would wonder whether he still held his position at the Instituto. Nor was it to be only his collaboration with Manuel that would draw him to Madrid. Unfortunately for the legend though fortunately for Antonio Machado, the poet was soon to learn that he could love again.

The first of the brothers' plays to be staged was an adaptation of Tirso de Molina's *El condenado por desconfiado*, rewritten by them in verse described as brilliant. The drama opened at the Teatro Español, Madrid, in January 1924. Just a year later *Hernani*, translated with Villaespesa so long ago, was produced and thereafter for half a dozen years or so the brothers had a play on the boards almost yearly. Most of their works were in both verse and prose; several were adaptations of plays by earlier writers, at times done with a third collaborator.

The high point of the Machados' career in the theatrical world was reached on November 8th, 1929, when the curtain was rung down on the opening night of *La Lola se va a los puertos*, an original play in verse. The brilliant Lola Membrives, who played the title role, and her company shared honors with the playwrights. For a while it seemed as though all Madrid was determined to celebrate their success. Ricardo Calvo did his share by restaging their *Juanillo Valcárcel* in which he and the incomparable María Guerrero had acted three years earlier. After this special performance, the Machados had to respond to endless curtain calls and they then discovered that Calvo had arranged for their praises to be sung by a number of poets. At this point Don Antonio probably mopped his brow. But the Duke of Amalfi, whom the Machados had first known as Antonio de Zayas, was among those poets and he and Calvo were the two "dear friends" to whom Antonio had dedicated his very first book.

Three weeks later the authors were fêted at an elaborate affair in the theatre where *Lola* was playing, and this was followed by yet another gathering, an intimate banquet at the Ritz Hotel for which José Antonio Primo de Rivera, son of the dictator, was one of the organizers as well as one of those delivering laudatory speeches.

Andalusian in spirit, with *coplas* and guitar music, grace, wit, and tragedy, the play has been performed many, many times since that electric first night. Some years ago it was made into a motion picture with Juanita Reina playing Lola.

The film crossed the ocean to the Americas, and in the United States, after having been shown before Spanish-speaking audiences, it made the rounds of the little theaters, this time with English subtitles. In 1950 Angel Barrios was awarded a prize of 50,000 pesetas for music he composed for *La Lola se va a los puertos*, the contest having been sponsored by the Ministry of National Education. The play, with the new music, was staged in Madrid and in Paris the following year. (Another composer, the Valencian Asíns Arbó, won the National Music Prize in 1950 for his *Seis canciones con palabras de Antonio Machado*.)

Nothing is known concerning the Machados' methods of working together; it was their custom to reply to any question on the matter that the best parts of any play had been written by the other. Certain it is, however, that Don Antonio was responsible for the development of the character of Lola and that he based his imaginary woman upon one of flesh and blood. In a letter to the still unknown "Guiomar" of his poems Antonio wrote, "Three years ago la Membrives asked us to write her an Andalusian play...Much of the first act was written before I knew you. The idea of sublimating Lola is mine. It occurred to me when I thought of my goddess..."[53] He promised to read the play to Guiomar and to erase and rewrite anything that did not please her.

From Antonio's poems and letters (which he did not date), we know that Guiomar had black hair, dusky-rose skin, feminine charm—and a halo. José Luis Cano, probably correctly, has deduced that Guiomar's first name was really Pilar.[54] She was the poet's dream incarnate:

> Like a streak of white light—
> only your form—
> in my dark night.
>
> And in the smooth sand
> beside the sea
> your dusky-rose flesh,
> Guiomar, suddenly!

71

In the gray of the wall,
prison and inn,
and in some future place
with only your voice and the wind . . .
(CLXXIV)

Antonio's love was reverent and idealized, no less so when their lives separated after almost ten years than in the beginning. Whatever the obstacle was that kept them from fulfillment, it presumably centered in the lady's household. Antonio liked best to think of Guiomar standing on her balcony, gowned in blue—but she did not wish him to walk past her house and once, when the poet had missed a meeting with her through some misunderstanding, he wrote to Guiomar that he had then walked "hurriedly" past her home, as though the haste mitigated the deed. He did not like to go to the theater when she might be there, for she would be surrounded by friends (a goddess among mortals to him) and he could not approach her. He respected her mind, listened to her opinions on the new poets, read his plays to her, and meekly promised to pay more attention to his grooming, explaining that he spent on books money that other men spent on their wardrobes.

Because other things were of real importance to him and clothes were not, Don Antonio quickly forgot these promises. When Darío Fernández-Florez was introduced to the poet at a gathering of artists and writers about this time, he noted the stained and wrinkled clothing, mentioning it in the written account of the meeting. A far more important element of Don Antonio's appearance interested him and he went on, "But his head had a rare, classic dignity, a solid, sculptured serenity, like a living statue."[55]

A personal advertisement, possibly inserted by Guiomar, was printed in *La gaceta literaria* (Madrid) on September 1st, 1930. Unsigned, it read: "ANTONIO MACHADO.—Are you in Segovia? We know nothing at all of you." Would his literary friends or his family have published such a notice? It gives a tinge of mystery and melodrama, as does the

72

elusive Guiomar, to the poet's Segovian years. "Their corner" seems to have been in a modest Madrid café. Guiomar visited him in his very respectable lodgings in Segovia and for the event he bought sheaves of rosemary and, the room being cold, placed a brazier near them on the little round table that still stands before the window.

All this was very different from Machado's relationship with Leonor; a gentle love and a heart-breaking pity pervaded his memories of his child-wife. It shocked his admirers to read in one of his letters to Guiomar that he had dreamed of their being married in the Church of Santa María la Mayor in Soria, the very church where his wedding actually had taken place. "We were kneeling together after the ceremony. There was an enormous crowd and the organ was playing. The dream was mixed with actual memories of my wedding, but with another difference: my spiritual state this time was one of overflowing joy, quite the contrary of that of my real-life wedding. The ceremony then was one of real martyrdom for me."[56] Perhaps it is not necessary to be shocked by this. He used the word "ceremony". An account of the nuptials in a Sorian newspaper reproved "the insane curiosity" exhibited by people who had gone to the church only because they had nothing better to do.[57] This is only a hint that there was unpleasantness of some kind; the account goes on to deplore the behavior of "certain ill-bred youths" who showed such lack of courtesy at the railroad station when the newly married couple were leaving Soria as to reflect upon the whole town. It could be that the trouble was instigated by youthful admirers of Leonor, for she was the object of teen-age infatuations, or it might have been mockery aimed at the bride and groom, so disparate in age and background. If the marriage remains incomprehensible, Antonio's unhappy recollections of the ceremony are at least explainable.

On December 9th, 1925, Antonio Machado y Ruiz was elected a corresponding member of The Hispanic Society of America. Less than two years later (March 24th, 1927), he was elected to the Real Academia Española to occupy the chair left vacant by Echegaray's death, his name having been proposed by Azorín, Ricardo León, and Palacio Valdés. Don Antonio never did take his seat because he never got around to completing his discourse and apparently did not even begin it until 1931. He had left Madrid by the time Manuel came across the manuscript, ink spotted, wine stained, burned by a constant smoker, and turned it over to José and Joaquín. It was published by the Hispanic Institute in the United States in 1949, apparently very nearly completed, in length approximately ten thousand words, and Guillermo de Torre has reprinted it.

Machado opened with an explanation of why he was unworthy of admittance to the Academia and then announced that his subject would be poetry. Most of what he had to say concerned European poetry of the nineteenth century and the first quarter of the twentieth—and, of course, he had thoughts on philosophy as well, considering it as he did a thing inseparable from poetry. The looking inward to the subjective—Machado himself exemplified the poet who does this—he regarded as "a modern invention...unknown to the Greeks...or to the men of the Renaissance," although he considered them no less human or profound than modern man.[58] Don Antonio quoted Heine's verses wherein he likened his own heart to a deep sea, moved by storm and tide but containing beautiful pearls hidden in the dark sand. The Spaniard approved the comparison, with the proviso that not all pearls are genuine. From Romanticism and the French Symbolists who "disintegrated" poetry, he went on to Proust and Joyce, asking in justification, "Is not a novel a lower type of poem?" What he had to say about these writers is interestingly phrased but he saw Proust as having put a final glorious period to a century of literature and Joyce as having entered a dead-end street, writing without logic or ethics. Contemporary French and Spanish poetry Machado pronounced disconcerting, even repelling, in its frigidity, naming only Paul Valéry and Jorge Guillén. As always, he

JOSÉ ORTEGA Y GASSET
By Joaquín Sorolla y Bastida
The Hispanic Society of America

MIGUEL DE UNAMUNO
By Ignacio Zuloaga y Zamora
The Hispanic Society of America

ANTONIO AND MANUEL MACHADO
In their playwriting years
Photo. Alfonso, Madrid

optimistically saw dawn about to break. In the section of his speech headed "Tomorrow", he foresaw great things, great poetry, the day when man would look at his neighbor with observing eyes, understanding him, feeling with him. The poet was reiterating the essence of his own writings.

Early in 1931 Antonio and Manuel were notified that Sevilla had made them "adopted sons" of the city. The next year Soria adopted Antonio. A ceremony took place in October during which the poet spoke and the new sign for the plaza near the Chapel of San Saturio, renamed in Machado's honor, was unveiled. Lines from *Campos de Soria* (CXIII) had been carved on rock; today they can be read on bronze plaques attached to the newly built walls outside the chapel. One of the speakers that day said that it would be impossible to know Soria without having read Machado's poems, and impossible to understand Machado without having seen Soria.

This may or may not be true. Soria did bring his inspiration to its highest wave, it gave him strength, fulfillment, and a bright anger that caused him to draw his poetical sword and lay about with a godlike fury. Yet Machado's powers of expression had been slowly maturing since the beginning of the century, his handling of words becoming the more masterful as he practised his art. He brought new beauties, simply expressed, to the language, revealing in many a line his own simplicity, the greatness of his heart, and the fathomless love he felt not only for Soria but for Spain. His evocation of the Castilian landscape remains unchallenged, and deep within himself the poet created a private landscape.

That poetry was to be the central core of Antonio Machado's being he had known very early. In the 1903 *Soledades* there is a poem (not in his *Obras*) ending:

> To the grave, slow accord of music and fragrance
> the old, the noble and sole cause of my prayer
> will lift with the delicate flight of a dove
> and the white word shall be raised to the altar there.

A surprising number of the elements that were to make up his poetic world appeared in that first slender volume. In a single poem (XXII) are found his labyrinthian roads and twisting paths, deep crypts of hopes and memories, chimeras. He has already heard the tears of old bells (XXV) and discovered in his dreams a vast labyrinth of mirrors (XXXVII). There is a seascape (XLIV) wherein the ocean bubbles and sings, swirls and laughs, and a single cryptic reference to the great body of water that signified so much in Machado's later work: "My old seas sleep" (XXIII). But the sea as his wonderful and all-encompassing symbol, charged with a multitude of meanings, was not yet evident in his poetry. It came to signify God, hope, life, death, and all things intangible.

By the time his second book appeared, golden bees had begun to buzz through Machado's verses, laboring in the secret galleries of his heart, in dreams and memories. Later they would flit through his thoughts and, most vividly, build a honeycomb within his heart from the bitterness they would find there.

A reference to "time" in the 1907 book shows the poet's pre-Bergsonian conception: "Yesterday is Never Again!" he said (LVII). It could be that he left the line in future editions as a reference to his youthful admiration for Poe and to the abrupt change in his thinking that resulted from his 1910 stay in Paris. Another line from this second book presages Machado's coming insight: he wrote of "macabre dancing in the presence of time" (LXXV).

Life—at least his own—he saw as a mirror, a sort of imitation of reality, and not even a mirror in good condition: "the mysterious quicksilver on the glass is blurred" (XLIX). Later he phrased it more graphically, seeing "a fatal hand scratching away at the quicksilver" (CXXXVI-xlix). In the poem to Azorín (CXLIII) he wrote: "And this vain hope/ of breaking the enchantment of the mirror!" It is a feeling that many have experienced, but it has occurred to no one else to express it in just this way.

76

Throughout Machado's poetry surely the words most frequently used are roads, pathways, streets, trails, and their concomitants, travelers, wayfarers, wanderers. "The traveler is the sum of the road," reads a line in one of his last poems (CLXIV. *Esto soñé*). In dreams he wanders through a maze of streets and alleys (or mirrors); man's thought is a crossroads exposed to the four winds (CLXI-LXIII); roads run through life, life itself is a pathway; every man must blaze his own trail and, in the end, must accept the fact that the pathway was opened upon the sea.

Deeply does he ponder on God, this man who was suspected of being an atheist, who wrote of his desire "to believe, believe, believe". He cannot keep God out of his verses. Machado has no ready-made prayers; the *saeta* of the religious procession fails to touch his heart; his thoughts on God are his own. The sea and God are Antonio Machado's ultimate symbols and the two are not only interchangeable, they are opposites and they are one.

> Every man has two
> battles to fight, for he
> must strive in dreams with God
> and waking, with the sea.
> (CXXXVI-XXVIII)

In a strange poem called *Profesión de fe* (CXXXVII-v) Don Antonio says: "God is not the sea, He is in the sea...He created the sea and is born/ of the sea like the cloud and the storm;/ He is the creator and the creature makes Him;/ His breath is the soul and through the soul He breathes./ I must make Thee, my God, as Thou madest me,/ and to give Thee the soul that Thou gavest me/ I must create Thee within myself."

Man dreams that "Death is an illusion of the sea" (CXXXVII-II); the poet yearns for a sea of forgetfulness (CLXIX); in his poem *A Julio Castro* (CLXIV) he says, "You live, I have been dreaming; but the sea, my brother, tempts us both." He advises in *Consejos:* "Know how to wait,

wait till the tide goes out...wait without leaving and always wait..." (CXXXVII-IV). When Frank O'Connor quoted the ending of this poem in *The mirror in the roadway*, a work on literature with a title that does not derive from Antonio Machado, he did not consider it necessary to name the author, complimenting Machado by saying casually, "As the Spanish poet puts it..."[59] In Rodolfo Halffter's piano solo, *Homenaje a Antonio Machado* (Mexico, 1940), the Spanish composer quotes all of *Consejos* as a prelude to the music.

Even his inspiration comes to this Spanish poet from the sea:

> From the ocean to the perception,
> from the perception to the conception,
> from the concept to the idea—
> oh, the beautiful chore!—
> from the idea to the sea.
> And then to begin once more!
>
> (CXXXVII-VIII)

Just before this poem comes a composition explaining how, like all men, the poet struggled within himself:

> Mind: "We'll never agree,
> O heart." And heart replies,
> hopefully, "We'll see."

In 1936, the year in which the fourth edition of Machado's complete poems was brought out, the first volume of his prose (interspersed with a few brief rhymes) was published under the title *Juan de Mairena*. Obviously written over a period of years, the book is filled with paradoxes, lit with humor, and frank as to opinions. Two sad events are clear: the poet and Guiomar had parted and war was breaking out in Spain.

Machado's mind ranges here and there: El Greco he describes as the explosion of Michelangelo; Shakespeare, he says admiringly, may be the unique example of the modern surpassing the ancient; Proust's famous book is the most interesting document of his time. The names of Perogrullo,

78

Manrique, Lope de Vega, Calderón, and other men of literature, as well as those of philosophers, are found throughout the volume. From his unfinished academy discourse Machado took the lines about Heine and translated the poetic passage he had been discussing.

Certain of man's basic goodness, Don Antonio pondered the fact that we can be quite capable of reading about battles wherein men die by the thousand, and of sleeping peacefully that night, yet be sadly troubled by witnessing the death of a dog, let alone of a fellow man—all for the lack of a little imagination.

Death, he goes on, is something we know nothing about. We may have seen someone die, but as long as he was in contact with us, the man was alive. "There is no one who can speak of the experience of death...Life, however, [is a different thing]...which explains the optimism of the Irishman in the tale who, launched into space from the sixth story, kept saying as he made his easy and ever swifter descent along the shortest route to the paving stones of the street: 'So far I'm all right.' "[60]

Philosophical thoughts are predominant. "There are men ...who go from poetry to philosophy; others who go from philosophy to poetry. What is inevitable is going from one to the other, in this as in everything."[61] A man must even doubt his own doubt. Should he declare that there is no truth, he is thereby inviting disbelief in the truth of that very statement. Antonio Machado was walking over bristly territory that had been crossed and recrossed by many an earlier philosopher.

His thoughts on some of the peoples of Europe are presented, although when he speaks of Russia, he refuses to accept Karl Marx. The Germans he characterizes as warlike. The Briton is a strangely civilized person: "No one but an Englishman is capable of smiling at his adversary and even of congratulating him for the master stroke that put an end to the combat."[62]

Leavening the earnest intention is a gentle chuckle, a

laugh turned usually upon the poet himself. He repeatedly cautions that he is not to be taken too seriously, and when he says that Juan de Mairena always keeps his watch twenty-four hours slow, he is not in much danger of being taken over-seriously. An innate horror of becoming pontifical causes the poet to deflate himself from time to time as in this bit of mockery: "When you read my book *On the essential heterogeneity of being* (in which 1800 pages of close-packed prose await you)..."[63] Advice meant for himself as well as for his fellow men is often in this vein: "Flee from stages, pulpits, platforms, and pedestals. Never lose contact with the ground; only thus will you have an approximate idea of your own stature."[64]

The book underlines the question of whether Don Antonio sometimes turned poetry into prose or whether his prose, entered first in private notebooks, was developed later in verse form. In the 1924 *Nuevas canciones* he had published a three-line poem (CLXI-xxiv):

> Slow, slow and painstaking:
> the making of things well
> matters more than the making.

Twelve years later Juan de Mairena is saying, "Between doing [or making] things well and doing them poorly is the compromise of not doing them at all."[65]

Not only has the discovery of Machado's *Complementarios* made it difficult to accept publication dates as being related to chronology of composition, the apparent development of the above thought from poetry to prose finds a contradiction in this very volume.

Near the beginning of the book a paragraph reads: "Blasphemy forms a part of popular religion. Distrust a people where they do not blaspheme: what is popular there is atheism. To ban blasphemy with more or less severe punitive laws is to envenom the heart of the people, making insincerity necessary in their talks with divinity. Will God, who reads hearts, let Himself by deceived? He will forgive first—

never doubt it—outspoken blasphemy rather than that kept hypocritically in the depths of the heart, or still more hypocritically, permuted to prayer."[66] Tucked into the volume more than a hundred pages farther along is a quatrain condensing this paragraph:

> There is blasphemy that is silent
> or converts itself to prayer.
> A different kind will spit at heaven,
> and God grants pardon there.
>
> (p.553)

The poet's prose is very revealing as to the man. By this time there could have been no more than a handful of literate Spaniards who did not know well the name of Antonio Machado. Today it is quite possible that he is more quoted than any other poet of Spain, though less widely known outside his own country than Lorca, whose plays are constantly in production. A subtle quality in Machado's quiet words, a certain inevitability in his phrasing, cause his lines to linger in the minds of men, while his dedication to Spain, his idealism, evoke a response in youthful hearts. An anthology of works by modern Spanish poets, leafed through at random, will reveal poem after poem either about Don Antonio or addressed to him, and there has even been one published entitled *A poem to the worn boots of Antonio Machado, Professor of French.*[67]

And by this time (1936) a great many changes had taken place within the country. King Alfonso had dismissed, after seven years, the dictator General Primo de Rivera whom he had set up in the spring of 1923. The peseta had been falling, there had been disorder in the streets, riots in the universities, practically all of which had been closed by the government at one time or another. Hunger was prevalent; danger, unrest, trouble were in the air. In mid-April 1931 the man who had been born a king fled his country. And Miguel de Unamuno, exiled in 1924, returned to his homeland the next day. In actuality, the sentence had been remitted years be-

81

fore, but Don Miguel, though he might cross the border for important occasions, had refused to stay overnight on Spanish territory as long as Alfonso sat on the throne.

Nicoleto Alcalá Zamora acted as Provisional President of the republic being born, and the first elections resulted in his becoming the official Chief of State. This was the man who had been Machado's opponent for that academic seat won but never occupied by Don Antonio.

With no liking for politics, Machado found himself drawn into fringe activities. "I need not excite myself over politics, either monarchical or republican," he wrote in one of his undated letters to Guiomar, and: "You are right, my goddess, when you tell me that the Republic—so desired!—I confess to having desired it sincerely—has disappointed us a little." [68] He was referring just then to the fact that Cataluña and the Basque Provinces were insisting upon immediate and absolute independence. Machado helped raise the republican tri-color at the Segovian town hall and for several days was among those responsible for maintaining order in the city under the new regime. Writing of this to Guiomar, he expressed his intention of remaining as completely apart from the republic as he had from the monarchy, an intention circumstances did not permit him to carry out.

Soon Professor Machado was transferred to the newly established Instituto de Calderón de la Barca in Madrid, where he went on teaching French. Tired, in poor health, aged beyond his years, dragging one leg when he walked, the poet said that he would be content if he could live for just two more years in order to prepare a definitive edition of his works.

Formidable were the problems facing the new government, particularly the complications and urgency of land reform and the existence of too many political parties, too many factions, all expecting an overnight miracle to be created especially for them. Leaders were often good men, sometimes lacking practical experience and frequently lacking the cunning of the expert politician. The world gasped with delight when writers and scholars were appointed ambassadors. The novelist Pérez de Ayala went to London, the brilliant Salvador de Madariaga to Washington. Plans were made for free education throughout the country and an ambitious program for building schools was set in force. García Lorca formed a traveling theatrical troupe called La Barraca and went out to tour the provinces, playing in the courtyards of inns as in the days of Lope de Vega. Under government auspices, Ricardo Marquina staged plays in towns and cities. It was Antonio Machado who suggested Marquina's name, and later that of his successor, Alejandro Casona.

By 1934 there was considerable dissatisfaction and dissension. A new cabinet was formed which, quite naturally, did not please all factions. Violent trouble broke out; the Asturian miners staged their desperate revolt, one incident touched off another, and by the summer of 1936 Spain was plunged into the greatest tragedy that can befall a nation, a civil war. Among the earliest victims was Lorca, brutally shot and probably buried in a ravine outside Granada, along with thousands of others.

Spain was turned into a training ground for foreign soldiers. Moors from North Africa were in the vanguard, under Spanish leadership. Hitler and Mussolini sent planes, bombs, guns, and conscripts to help one side. An international brigade of idealists, adventurers, and opportunists arrived to help the other; France gave some aid; Russia furnished not only men and matériel but huge posters of Stalin which were plastered around Madrid. Don Antonio, born and bred a republican, felt distaste for Karl Marx and his doctrines which were, he said, pure cynicism. "With Marx, gentlemen," said Juan de Mairena, "Europe, barely Christianized, is retrogressing to the Old Testament." [69]

When, in November of 1936, with the capital under siege, the government was forced to move to Valencia, thought was given to the gentle poet who labored in his own way for the republic. Léon-Felipe and Rafael Alberti were charged with the responsibility of persuading Antonio Machado to

83

follow the government to safety. He finally did agree, provided that his mother, along with José and Joaquín and their families (the children, of all ages, totaled eight), might go with him. They were evacuated to Rocafort, outside Valencia, where they were given a house with a pleasant garden. Daily the poet would climb to the top of a tower from which the sea was visible. In the afternoon he might give French or English lessons to his brothers' children, although his own grasp of the latter tongue was limited to a reading knowledge. By night, unless bombardments made a blackout compulsory, his window would be a bright square until four or even five o'clock. It was on a night when Valencia was being mercilessly bombarded that Don Antonio wrote several sonnets, among them *La muerte del niño herido* (page 853).

Friends would come from the city for Sunday visits. Ricardo Calvo, on his way out of the country, stopped off at Rocafort to see his old friend for what turned out to be the last time. Rafael Ferreres and other young poets came repeatedly, bringing cigarettes when they could. High officials and simple workers visited him. Don Antonio himself seldom ventured into the city, twenty minutes or so away by electric train, unless he felt the urge to purchase books or had reluctantly agreed to read his poetry or give a talk. Once, in accordance with the government's desire, Don Antonio made the trip in order to deliver a speech before a large crowd. Even to mount the platform he needed help. His physical strength was ebbing, and it took all his moral strength as well to address that multitude.

Though less frequently inspired to write poetry in those days, Don Antonio did compose a few war poems, some of which have never been included in any book, and he wrote some enchanting lines on Valencia of the slender towers and delicate nights. He thought of Guiomar, and wrote verses to her. She had left Spain; Machado did not know her whereabouts nor had he any way of knowing that she had been trying in vain to reëstablish contact with him. The poet awoke one dawn, having dreamed of searching for Guiomar through a labyrinth of twisting, turning streets and alleys. He missed her inspiration: "Without a woman/ there is no fertility or knowledge."[70] Insisting to his public that the lady was purely imaginary, he wrote from his heart, in that sonnet called *La muerte del niño herido:* "Thy memory, it hurts me, goddess mine." The clever little machine that manufactured poems was supposed to have produced this *copla*, which now had a vivid personal application:

> If a man hears not his name
> on the lips of a woman, they claim
> no man is he.
> This could be.

> (p.410)

Another that he must have written himself although he termed it a popular Andalusian *copla*—"or so it seems to me," he said cryptically—reads:

> I have a pain, a pain
> so great I would almost agree
> that I do not have the pain:
> rather, the pain has me.

> (p.719)

During the war years most of Don Antonio's work was prose credited to Juan de Mairena and published in the republican *Hora de España*. When Unamuno died on the last day of December 1936, Machado wrote about the passing of his friend, saying with all truth that no man had ever lived less reconciled to the idea of his own death.[71] This attitude, the heart of Unamuno's "tragic sense of life", was the antithesis of Machado's air of being half in love with death, of contemplating its inevitability with a gentle wonder.

After fifteen months in Valencia, the Machados were once more evacuated, this time to Barcelona where they and other refugees were given shelter in the Torre de Castañer on the Paseo de San Gervasio, a stately nineteenth-century building with windows overlooking the sea, its garden walls colorful with still lifes. The escutcheon on the gates, the chapel in which the poet's elderly mother prayed daily, the family pantheon, give a feeling of history and permanence. The house then impressed its residents as large, cold, and shadow-filled, "with garrets from a novel by Baroja".[72] A great many mirrors in gold frames were hung about; Don Antonio saw himself in multiple reflections, as though his dreams had been prescient. Friends gathered around, and the poet is described as telling amusing anecdotes and laughing often, huddled under a blanket, a small brazier at his feet. Often the lights would go out, signifying a threatened attack; the conversation would continue with no change of tone. Food was not plentiful, the cold was piercing, tobacco was nonexistent. Don Antonio continued to write, publishing articles in Barcelona's daily paper, *La vanguardia espa-ñola*, and elsewhere. The last book of his to be published during his lifetime was *La tierra de Alvargonzález y can-ciones del alto Duero*, printed in Barcelona in 1938.

On the twenty-second of January 1939, with Barcelona about to fall, Señora Ruiz de Machado, Antonio, and José and his wife left the city in a car forming a small part of a convoy heading for France. José has described the exodus in detail. There was a three-day pause in Cerviá del Ter, north of Gerona, after which the convoy started up again, the best seats going to the agile ones who needed them least. There was another overnight stop at an old country house where there was no room for anyone to lie down. The bitter chill, fear of bombs, sadness, kept people (including close friends of the Machados) pacing nervously about all night long in a nightmarish effect. The journey was continued with frequent stops when planes threatened overhead; the passengers would alight to seek what cover they could, with Don Antonio always last to leave the car. Their gasoline ran out and a member of the militia had the tank filled for them, proud of the opportunity to be of help to the thin, tired, elderly man who was Antonio Machado. The trek was continued on a road strewn with abandoned luggage and cars; eventually the road became so choked that driving was literally impossible.

In the dark, with a torrential rain falling, the four Machados left their vehicle, of necessity abandoning their luggage, including books that Don Antonio had struggled to keep, and certain papers. The poet looked sadly at his little mother, noting the white hair being driven against her temples by the same rain that rolled down her lovely cheeks like tears. On the night of January twenty-seventh they entered France near Cerbère. A friend obtained a car for them but when it arrived only one seat was available. Antonio took his mother on his knees; the rest of the party walked. Even a cup of coffee was unobtainable in Cerbère, Spanish currency being unacceptable. The Spaniards watched with horror the putting into effect of the solution France had decided would best serve in her emergency. Children were separated from parents, wives from husbands; they would be put into separate camps behind barbed wire. José considers it a miracle that the little party escaped this fate. Thanks to the efforts of "a good friend, an illustrious professor", they were allowed, after hours of waiting on a windy station platform, to enter a box car and spend the night, however uncomfortably, sheltered.

The next day, the group walked to Collioure, very near the border. As they were entering the town Don Antonio's mother whispered, "Will we be in Sevilla soon?"[73] They found grateful refuge at last in the Hotel Quignol-Quintana. The kindly hotel people had French and Spanish blood; they recognized the name of Antonio Machado. The secretary of the Spanish Embassy at Paris, a friend of Don Antonio's, supplied him with funds.

Collioure would not have seemed attractive to the Spaniards then, but it is a colorful fishing hamlet on a blue bay of the Mediterranean, long a favorite haunt of painters. Derain, Matisse, Spanish artists, English water colorists, have brought their easels to the seaside town. Its crescent beach, sheltered from the wind, is not too unpleasant even in February, with the blue waves rolling in, a "Roman" tower rising on one side and, opposite, a Knights Templars castle standing on an eminence. The town is a jumble of little balconied and shuttered houses, white, pink, yellow, green. Small and homelike, the hotel overlooks the village square where men gather, clad in blouses and trousers of French blue, sometimes red-sashed, and where the town crier makes his announcements at close of day. The beach is not far from the hotel; no farther away in the opposite direction is the town cemetery.

Within a day or two Don Antonio, weak and thin, was standing at his window watching the activities down in the square, and making the effort to go downstairs to the hotel dining room for his simple meals. Twice he persuaded José to walk with him to the beach. Wind ruffled Antonio's hair as he stared long at the sea. "From arcane sea we come, to unknown sea we go..." he had written. The blue bay, that last bit of sea water glimpsed by Machado, inspired Eugenio Florit to compose a tender little poem entitled *Collioure:*

> Mar francesito de Matisse
> entre tus pinos asomado;
> eres más que eso para mí,
> mar español de Antonio Machado.

It was on February twenty-second that Spain's poet died. The last words on his lips were "Adios, madre." Manuel, then in Burgos, learned of his brother's death in a brutal fashion when, in a casual barbershop encounter, a man asked him, "Are you by any chance related to that poet, Antonio Machado, who died in France yesterday?"[74]

The funeral services for Don Antonio were of a laic nature, with Collioure's mayor saying a few words. A generous family of Collioure had offered to bury the poet in their family vault, an offer accepted with gratitude by José. Señora Machado had been too ill—small wonder!—to be aware of the death of her favorite son; the knowledge came to her suddenly in her own last hours, three days later. And now the French family wished to have the mother buried with her son. The tombs were never faced with marble nor

88

carved; time and weather were hard on them. A small marble plaque that was carved and hung on Don Antonio's niche eventually stood on the ground, cracked and misshapen. Townspeople were likely to leave a spray of flowers on it when they passed by, flowers that came from nearby fields. Visitors made a shrine of the modest tomb. Pilgrimages came from Spain; in 1945 Jean Cassou paid homage, leaving offerings of laurel and everlastings. Immediately upon hearing of Antonio Machado's death, Cassou had requested José's permission to arrange a ceremonious funeral in the French capital, an offer the younger brother declined, knowing well that the simple cemetery in Collioure would have been Antonio's own preference. The hotel where Machado died recalls his brief presence with a plaque carved by the Catalan Joan Rebull who, it was hoped, would one day be the sculptor to design a monument to the poet.

During recent years many have been moved to honor the Spanish poet in various countries and in various ways. The plaque commemorating his birthplace was unveiled at the Palacio de las Dueñas in April 1952, at which ceremony José María Pemán spoke on the appropriate theme of the lemon tree and the fountain in Machado's poetry. There have been *homenajes* in a number of countries and in many cities of Spain, more or less like the 1952 International Congress of Poetry which met in Don Antonio's Segovian room and read his poems aloud, with his former pupil, the poet Alfonso Moreno, taking part, and that organized at Baeza in May 1954 when young poets, among them Ramón de Garciasol, read poems by Machado. As an act of homage in Paris, an exhibition of works of Spanish artists was held at the Maison de la Pensée in February 1955. Antonio Machado appeared in sculpture and on canvas; Juan Sáez Huerta showed a painting called *The Crime was in Granada*, the title of Machado's poem on the death of Lorca; Picasso's conception of the poet appeared on the catalogue cover.

The Swedish Royal Academy, awarding the 1956 Nobel Prize for Literature to Juan Ramón Jiménez, announced

89

that it was honoring also, and to equal extent, Antonio Machado and Federico García Lorca.

Sevilla expressed the desire to have the bones of the poet returned to his birthplace to be interred in a pantheon for famous Sevillians. Sorians were desirous of having him reburied with Leonor in a splendid sepulcher to be built on Don Antonio's beloved Castilian plain. The mayor of Madrid proposed that a monument be raised in Machado's honor and placed in one of the public parks of the capital, and at Collioure it was suggested that Emiliano Barral's bust of the poet might fittingly be placed on a pedestal in the little cemetery.

Late in 1957 the Academia Española de la Lengua officially announced its interest in arranging to have Machado's remains brought back to his homeland, but the following summer an organization called Les Amis de Antonio Machado, which for more than a decade had been raising funds in Europe and in Hispanic America for the erection of a tomb in the Collioure cemetery for both the poet and his mother, achieved its object. The Spanish 'cellist, Pablo Casals, and Frenchmen of the caliber of Malraux, Cassou, Sartre, and the recent Nobel Prize winner, Albert Camus, were among those who, having loved Antonio Machado for himself or for his poetry (or both), had devoted time and effort toward furtherance of the project. The town itself gave the plot. When the remains of Don Antonio and his mother were transferred on July 16th, 1958, in the presence of mourners famous and unknown, the flowers that were tenderly placed on the new tomb (on behalf of Marcel Bataillon) were wild flowers from the Guadarramas.

The twentieth anniversary of Machado's death evoked a wave of public tributes to the poet's memory. At Málaga, José Luis Cano gave a talk. At Soria, Heliodoro Carpintero, occupant of the "Antonio Machado Chair" at the Instituto, spoke, as did Julián Marías, author of the account of Machado and his works in the *Diccionario de literatura española*. Notable was the *homenaje* at Segovia, which took place in the patio of the house where Don Antonio had lived. The crowd that assembled in that small area included hundreds from out of town, due to the fact that an appeal signed by seventy-five Spanish leaders—scholars like Ramón Menéndez Pidal, creative writers like José Cela, men of learning and eminence like Gregorio Marañón—had suggested attendance at the Segovian homage for those Spaniards who could not get up to Collioure. Dionisio Ridruejo, the poet who had grown up in Segovia and whose ideals of life and literature had been absorbed in Professor Machado's classroom, as well as Pedro Laín Entralgo, the brilliant doctor-scholar-writer, and others, read poems by Machado or talked about him and his work.

Within a few days further ceremonies were celebrated at the Sorbonne, arranged by Marcel Bataillon and Charles Vincent Aubrun, both noted Hispanists, with Picasso once again lending his talents by designing the poster. The University of Madrid, too, celebrated the memory of a poet who had entered her doors, in full maturity, to earn his doctoral degree. Luis Felipe Vivanco, who has studied Machado's works, was among the speakers.

The quiet tribute rendered in the Collioure cemetery on February 22nd, 1959, attracted Spaniards and Frenchmen. Among the former group, which included young writers now coming into prominence—José Agustín Goytisolo and Blas de Otero, for example—a feeling existed that they represented the many Spaniards who would have liked to attend but could not. They came bearing wreaths of flowers and a wooden chest filled with Spanish earth. Many of the younger generation respond to the idealism in Machado's life and poems. Like his, their hearts are warm with love for their motherland, their minds lit by love of poetry; like him, they are creative and alive—for Antonio Machado, whose bones lie in Collioure, is alive today.

91

Antonio Machado (signature)

Selected Poems

———

With Translations

VII

El limonero lánguido suspende
una pálida rama polvorienta,
sobre el encanto de la fuente limpia,
y allá en el fondo sueñan
los frutos de oro . . .

                Es una tarde clara,
casi de primavera,
tibia tarde de marzo,
que el hálito de abril cercano lleva;
y estoy solo, en el patio silencioso,
buscando una ilusión cándida y vieja:
alguna sombra sobre el blanco muro,
algún recuerdo, en el pretil de piedra
de la fuente dormido, o, en el aire,
algún vagar de túnica ligera.

En el ambiente de la tarde flota
ese aroma de ausencia,
que dice al alma luminosa: nunca,
y al corazón: espera.

Ese aroma que evoca los fantasmas
de las fragancias vírgenes y muertas.

Sí, te recuerdo, tarde alegre y clara,
casi de primavera,
tarde sin flores, cuando me traías
el buen perfume de la hierbabuena,
y de la buena albahaca,
que tenía mi madre en sus macetas.

Que tú me viste hundir mis manos puras
en el agua serena,
para alcanzar los frutos encantados
que hoy en el fondo de la fuente sueñan . . .

Sí, te conozco, tarde alegre y clara,
casi de primavera.

VII

Lazily the lemon tree suspends
a bough of dusty pallor, leaning
over the bright enchantment of the fountain
where in the depths lie dreaming
fruit of gold . . .

           A brilliant afternoon
with springtime very near,
a mild afternoon of March,
wafting the breath of nearby April here;
and I am alone in the quietness of the patio,
seeking an old and very naive illusion:
a shadow cast on the whiteness of the wall,
some memory hid in the circling rail of stone
around the sleeping fount, or in the air,
the whisper of a diaphanous garment blown.

In the atmosphere of the afternoon a hint
of absence lightly floats,
saying this to the luminous mind: "Never,"
but telling the heart, "Hope."

It brings to memory long-gone fragrances,
virginal, dead, of unsubstantial ghosts.

Yes, I recall you, bright, gay afternoon
with springtime very near,
a day when, lacking flowers, you brought to me
the peppermint's fresh and sparkling clean perfume
and that of potted sweet basil
nurtured by my mother to bloom.

You saw me plunge my young and guileless hands
in waters cool
to gather up in them the enchanted fruit
dreaming again today in the depths of the pool . . .

Indeed I know you, gay, bright afternoon
with springtime almost here.

                         A. W. F.

IX
(ORILLAS DEL DUERO)

Se ha asomado una cigüeña a lo alto del campanario.
Girando en torno a la torre y al caserón solitario,
ya las golondrinas chillan. Pasaron del blanco invierno,
de nevascas y ventiscas los crudos soplos de infierno.

Es una tibia mañana.
El sol calienta un poquito la pobre tierra soriana.

Pasados los verdes pinos,
casi azules, primavera
se ve brotar en los finos
chopos de la carretera
y del río. El Duero corre, terso y mudo, mansamente.
El campo parece, más que joven, adolescente.

Entre las hierbas alguna humilde flor ha nacido,
azul o blanca. ¡Belleza del campo apenas florido,
y mística primavera!

¡Chopos del camino blanco, álamos de la ribera,
espuma de la montaña
ante la azul lejanía,
sol del día, claro día!
¡Hermosa tierra de España!

XI

Yo voy soñando caminos
de la tarde. ¡Las colinas
doradas, los verdes pinos,
las polvorientas encinas! . . .
¿Adónde el camino irá?
Yo voy cantando, viajero
a lo largo del sendero . . .

IX

BANKS OF THE DUERO

A stork on top of the belfry, high above the ground,
has shown itself, and swallows, screaming, circle round
tower and lonely building. The harsh, infernal blasts
of winter, stormy winds, and blizzards, now have passed.

It is a morning mild and bland.
The sun gently warms the poor Sorian land.

Beyond the blue-green splendor
of distant pine, one sees
spring budding in the slender
roadside poplar trees
and those on riverbank. The Duero, smooth, acquiescent,
runs through a countryside, rather than young, adolescent.

The birth of some humble flower in grasses is revealed
in blue or white. Beauty of sparsely flowering field
and mystical springtide!

Dark the roadside poplars, white by the riverside;
on faroff blue the stain
of the mountain's frothy spray;
sun of the day, the brilliant day.
Beautiful land of Spain!

A. McV.

XI

I dream of roads that go
toward sunset. Green of pines,
hills with a golden glow,
live oaks in dusty lines.
Where is the end of the way?
As I go, I sing my song
all the road along . . .

97

—La tarde cayendo está—.
"En el corazón tenía
"la espina de una pasión;
"logré arrancármela un día:
"ya no siento el corazón".

Y todo el campo un momento
se queda, mudo y sombrío,
meditando. Suena el viento
en los álamos del río.

La tarde más se obscurece;
y el camino que serpea
y débilmente blanquea,
se enturbia y desaparece.

Mi cantar vuelve a plañir:
"Aguda espina dorada,
"quién te pudiera sentir
"en el corazón clavada".

XIII

Hacia un ocaso radiante
caminaba el sol de estío,
y era, entre nubes de fuego, una trompeta gigante,
tras de los álamos verdes de las márgenes del río.

Dentro de un olmo sonaba la sempiterna tijera
de la cigarra cantora, el monorritmo jovial,
entre metal y madera,
que es la canción estival.

En una huerta sombría,
giraban los cangilones de la noria soñolienta.
Bajo las ramas obscuras el son del agua se oía.
Era una tarde de julio, luminosa y polvorienta.

It is the end of day.
"A thorn of passion in
my heart was lodged. I tore
it out one day and then
I felt my heart no more."

The land a moment lies
with the still and sombre look
of thought. A light wind sighs
in the poplars by the brook.

Deeper the twilight grows
and the road that turns and veers
and feebly, whitely shows,
darkens and disappears.

My song goes on in pain,
"O sharp and golden spine,
to feel you once again
piercing this heart of mine."

B. G. P.

XIII

Toward a radiant west
traveled the summer sun,
and it was, among the fiery clouds, a giant trumpet
behind the verdant poplars on the riverbank.

Within an elm tree sounded the sempiternal scissors
of the minstrel cicada, the merry monorhythm,
between metal and wood,
that makes the estival song.

In the midst of shadowy orchards
the buckets of a dreaming water wheel were turning.
Under darkening branches, the sound of the water was heard.
An evening it was in July, luminous and dusty.

Yo iba haciendo mi camino,
absorto en el solitario crepúsculo campesino.

Y pensaba: "¡Hermosa tarde, nota de la lira inmensa
toda desdén y armonía;
hermosa tarde, tú curas la pobre melancolía
de este rincón vanidoso, obscuro rincón que piensa!"

Pasaba el agua rizada bajo los ojos del puente.
Lejos la ciudad dormía,
como cubierta de un mago fanal de oro trasparente.
Bajo los arcos de piedra el agua clara corría.

Los últimos arreboles coronaban las colinas
manchadas de olivos grises y de negruzcas encinas.
Yo caminaba cansado,
sintiendo la vieja angustia que hace el corazón pesado.

El agua en sombra pasaba tan melancólicamente,
bajo los arcos del puente,
como si al pasar dijera:

"Apenas desamarrada
la pobre barca, viajero, del árbol de la ribera,
se canta: no somos nada.
Donde acaba el pobre río la inmensa mar nos espera".

Bajo los ojos del puente pasaba el agua sombría.
(Yo pensaba: ¡el alma mía!)

Y me detuve un momento,
en la tarde, a meditar . . .
¿Qué es esta gota en el viento
que grita al mar: soy el mar?

Vibraba el aire asordado
por los élitros cantores que hacen el campo sonoro,
cual si estuviera sembrado
de campanitas de oro.

I walked, broaching a path,
absorbed in the lonely twilight of the countryside.

And I thought, "O lovely evening, note from that great lyre,
all disdain and harmony;
lovely evening, how you heal poor melancholy
in this proud remoteness, this dark and thoughtful corner."

The water curled, passing under the arcs of the bridge.
Faroff the city slept
under a magic dome of gold transparency.
Beneath arches of stone bright was the water flowing.

The final flaming skies were crowning sloping hills,
gray with olive trees, black with encina oaks.
Weary, I walked on,
feeling the old anguish that makes the heart grow weary.

So mournful was the water, flowing toward the shadows
under the arcs of the bridge
as though to say in passing:

"Scarce, O wayfarer, had
the poor little bark been loosed from the tree on the riverbank
than a song arose: 'We are naught.
Where the poor river ends, the wide sea awaits us.' "

Under the eyes of the bridge flowed the shadowy water.
(I could but think: My very soul!)

And I stopped myself a moment
in the dusk, to meditate:
What is this drop on the wind
that cries to the sea, "I am the sea!"?

The air quivered, deafened
by insect elytra making fields ring out with sound
as though they had been sown
with little bells of gold.

En el azul fulguraba
un lucero diamantino.
Cálido viento soplaba
alborotando el camino.

Yo, en la tarde polvorienta,
hacia la ciudad volvía.
Sonaban los cangilones de la noria soñolienta.
Bajo las ramas obscuras caer el agua se oía.

XIV
(CANTE HONDO)

Yo meditaba absorto, devanando
los hilos del hastío y la tristeza,
cuando llegó a mi oído,
por la ventana de mi estancia, abierta

a una caliente noche de verano,
el plañir de una copla soñolienta,
quebrada por los trémolos sombríos
de las músicas magas de mi tierra.

. . . Y era el Amor, como una roja llama . . .
—Nerviosa mano en la vibrante cuerda
ponía un largo suspirar de oro,
que se trocaba en surtidor de estrellas—.

. . . Y era la Muerte, al hombro la cuchilla,
el paso largo, torva y esquelética.
—Tal cuando yo era niño la soñaba—.

Y en la guitarra, resonante y trémula,
la brusca mano, al golpear, fingía
el reposar de un ataúd en tierra.

Y era un plañido solitario el soplo
que el polvo barre y la ceniza avienta.

Dazzling in the blue
shone the diamond star;
warm the wind was blowing,
stirring up the path.

I, in dusty eventide,
cityward then turned.
The buckets of the dreaming water wheel were splashing.
Under darkening branches the falling water was heard.

A. McV.

XIV

DEEP SONG

While deep in thought I sat absorbed,
winding the endless skeins of care
and tedium, there came
through my window open to the air,

hot in the summer night, a ballad
broken with sombre tremolos,
dreamy notes of a song,
the haunting music my country knows.

. . . And it was Love, a flame of red . . .
On the vibrant string his nervous stroke
brought forth a golden sigh—
a fountain-rain of stars, it broke.

And it was Death, scythe on shoulder,
a skeleton grim and stepping slow,
just as I saw him in childhood dreams.

On the resonant, tremulous guitar
his hand would strike the sudden blow
of a coffin dropped in spade-cut ground.

And it was wind that blows the dust
and winnows ashes with mournful sound.

H. E. F.

XVI

Siempre fugitiva y siempre
cerca de mí, en negro manto
mal cubierto el desdeñoso
gesto de tu rostro pálido.
No sé adónde vas, ni dónde
tu virgen belleza tálamo
busca en la noche. No sé
qué sueños cierran tus párpados,
ni de quien haya entreabierto
tu lecho inhospitalario.
. . . .
Detén el paso, belleza
esquiva, detén el paso.

Besar quisiera la amarga,
amarga flor de tus labios.

XXI

Daba el reloj las doce . . . y eran doce
golpes de azada en tierra . . .
. . . ¡Mi hora!—grité— . . . El silencio
me respondió:—No temas;
tú no verás caer la última gota
que en la clepsidra tiembla.

Dormirás muchas horas todavía
sobre la orilla vieja,
y encontrarás una mañana pura
amarrada tu barca a otra ribera.

104

XVI

Forever fugitive and ever
near me somewhere, robed in black,
disdain upon your pallid features
scarcely hidden, there intact.
I know not where you go, nor where
within the night your virgin beauty
seeks a bridal bed. Nor what
the dreams that come to close your lids,
nor yet for whom you have prepared
your most inhospitable bed.
. . . .
Pause a moment, hostile beauty,
slow your steps.

I long to kiss the bitter,
bitter flower of your lips.

A. McV.

XXI

The clock struck twelve . . . and twelve they were,
the blows of a spade on earthen plot.
"My hour!" I cried . . . The silence
answered me, "Fear not;
you shall not see the last drop fall
that trembles in the water clock.

"On the familiar bank will you find sleep
for many hours more,
and one bright morning shall you find
your bark fast moored to the other shore."

XXII

Sobre la tierra amarga,
caminos tiene el sueño
laberínticos, sendas tortuosas,
parques en flor y en sombra y en silencio;

criptas hondas, escalas sobre estrellas;
retablos de esperanzas y recuerdos.
Figurillas que pasan y sonríen
—juguetes melancólicos de viejo—;

imágenes amigas,
a la vuelta florida del sendero,
y quimeras rosadas
que hacen camino . . . lejos . . .

XXIV

El sol es un globo de fuego,
la luna es un disco morado.

Una blanca paloma se posa
en el alto ciprés centenario.

Los cuadros de mirtos parecen
de marchito velludo empolvado.

¡El jardín y la tarde tranquila! . . .
Suena el agua en la fuente de mármol.

XXII

Over the bitter earth
the dream has its roads
labyrinthian, with tortuous paths,
parks in flower, in shadow, and in silence;

deep-set crypts and stairways over stars;
the backdrop, scenes of hopes and memories.
Little figures passing by and smiling—
melancholy toys of olden times—

friendly images
at the flowering turn of the path,
and rose-colored chimeras
that open a road . . . afar . . .

A. McV.

XXIV

The sun is a globe of fire,
the moon is a purple disk.

A white dove is alighting
in the tall centenary cypress.

The squares of myrtles seem
parchment faded and dusty.

Garden and tranquil evening!
Water splashes in the marble fountain.

A. McV.

XXV

¡Tenue rumor de túnicas que pasan
sobre la infértil tierra! ...
¡Y lágrimas sonoras
de las campanas viejas!

Las ascuas mortecinas
del horizonte humean ...
Blancos fantasmas lares
van encendiendo estrellas.

—Abre el balcón. La hora
de una ilusión se acerca ...
La tarde se ha dormido,
y las campanas sueñan.

XXVII

La tarde todavía
dará incienso de oro a tu plegaria,
y quizás el cenit de un nuevo día
amenguará tu sombra solitaria.

Mas no es tu fiesta el Ultramar lejano,
sino la ermita junto al manso río;
no tu sandalia el soñoliento llano
pisará, ni la arena del hastío.

Muy cerca está, romero,
la tierra verde y santa y florecida
de tus sueños; muy cerca, peregrino
que desdeñas la sombra del sendero
y el agua del mesón en tu camino.

XXV

Tenuous murmur of garments drifting by
over infertile land! . . .
And the sound of musical tears
shed by ancient bells!

Dying embers are smoking
on the far horizon.
White ghosts of hearthside gods
are lighting up the stars.

Open the balcony window.
Illusion's hour draws near.
The day has fallen asleep
and the bells are dreaming.

A. McV.

XXVII

The evening yet may
grant a golden incense to thy prayer
and perhaps the zenith of a newer day
diminish thy solitary shadow there.

Not thine the fiesta overseas, instead,
the hermitage beside the quiet stream;
thine is not the sandal that will tread
the drowsy plain nor tedious desert scene.

Near, O pilgrim, hath
it come, the green, the holy, flowering land
thou knowest in dreams; nearer, traveler, aye,
for thou heedest not the shade across thy path
nor the water of the inn along the way.

A. McV.

XXVIII

Crear fiestas de amores
en nuestro amor pensamos,
quemar nuevos aromas
en montes no pisados,

y guardar el secreto
de nuestros rostros pálidos,
porque en las bacanales de la vida
vacías nuestras copas conservamos,
mientras con eco de cristal y espuma
ríen los zumos de la vid dorados.
. . . .
Un pájaro escondido entre las ramas
del parque solitario,
silba burlón . . .
Nosotros exprimimos
la penumbra de un sueño en nuestro vaso . . .
Y algo, que es tierra en nuestra carne, siente
la humedad del jardín como un halago.

XXIX

Arde en tus ojos un misterio, virgen
esquiva y compañera.

No sé si es odio o es amor la lumbre
inagotable de tu aljaba negra.

Conmigo irás mientras proyecte sombra
mi cuerpo y quede a mi sandalia arena.

—¿Eres la sed o el agua en mi camino?
Dime, virgen esquiva y compañera.

110

XXVIII

To create fiestas of loves
within our love we plan,
to burn new fragrances
on untrodden mountains,

and to shield the secret
of our pallid faces,
for here amidst the bacchanals of life
always empty must we keep our glasses,
while with echoes of crystal and of froth
the juices of the golden vines are laughing.
. . . .
A bird hidden within the lonely park,
somewhere among the branches,
whistles mockery . . .
          The while we press
the shadow of a dream within our glass . . .
And something of earth within our flesh feels
the dampness of the garden like a caress.
                          A. McV.

XXIX

A mystery burns within your eyes, elusive
virgin, my companion.

I know not whether it is hate or love,
the inexhaustible flame within your quiver's blackness.

You will go with me while my body projects
a shadow, and while sand clings to my sandal.

—Are you the thirst or the water on my road?
Tell me, elusive virgin, my companion.
                          A. McV.

XXXII

Las ascuas de un crepúsculo morado
detrás del negro cipresal humean...
En la glorieta en sombra está la fuente
con su alado y desnudo Amor de piedra,
que sueña mudo. En la marmórea taza
reposa el agua muerta.

XLI

Me dijo una tarde
de la primavera:
Si buscas caminos
en flor en la tierra,
mata tus palabras
y oye tu alma vieja.
Que el mismo albo lino
que te vista, sea
tu traje de duelo,
tu traje de fiesta.
Ama tu alegría
y ama tu tristeza,
si buscas caminos
en flor en la tierra.
Respondí a la tarde
de la primavera:
Tú has dicho el secreto
que en mi alma reza:
yo odio la alegría
por odio a la pena.
Mas antes que pise
tu florida senda,
quisiera traerte
muerta mi alma vieja.

XXXII

The embers of a purple twilight
smoke behind black cypress trees.
A fountain in the shadowed arbor
bears a nude stone Love with wings,
a silent dreamer. Lifeless water
rests within the marble basin.

J. R. L.

XLI

It was a spring afternoon
that I heard speak:
"If blossoming paths
on earth you seek,
kill then your words,
your old heart construe;
let that same white suit
you are wearing do
for your mourning clothes
and your gala dress;
embrace both joy
and unhappiness
if blossoming paths
you seek on your way."
And I replied
to the springtime day,
"Thus have you told
my secret prayer:
I do dread joy,
for I hate despair.
Before on your flowering
path I tread
let me bring unto you
my aged heart—dead."

A. McV.

LIV

(LOS SUEÑOS MALOS)

Está la plaza sombría;
muere el día.
Suenan lejos las campanas.

De balcones y ventanas
se iluminan las vidrieras,
con reflejos mortecinos,
como huesos blanquecinos
y borrosas calaveras.

En toda la tarde brilla
una luz de pesadilla.
Está el sol en el ocaso.
Suena el eco de mi paso.

—¿Eres tú? Ya te esperaba ...
—No eras tú a quien yo buscaba.

LX

¿Mi corazón se ha dormido?
Colmenares de mis sueños
¿ya no labráis? ¿Está seca
la noria del pensamiento,
los cangilones vacíos,
girando, de sombra llenos?

No, mi corazón no duerme.
Está despierto, despierto.
Ni duerme ni sueña, mira,
los claros ojos abiertos,
señas lejanas y escucha
a orillas del gran silencio.

L I V

EVIL DREAMS

In shade the plaza lies
while daylight dies.
Bells sound faroff melodies.

On windows and on balconies
illumination glows
with reflections dull
as murky skulls
or whitened bones.

Over all the evening streams
a light of evil dreams.
Low is the sun in the west.
Echo follows my steps.

"Is it you? I have waited our meeting."
"But it was not you I was seeking."

A. McV.

L X

Can my heart have gone to sleep?
Apiaries of my dreams,
have you stopped your labors? Has
the water wheel of thought run dry,
do its empty buckets keep
whirling, whirling, shadow-filled?

No, my heart is not asleep.
It is awake, it is awake.
It neither sleeps nor dreams, but looks
with open eyes and vision deep
at distant signals, and it listens
to the shores of the great silence.

J. R. L.

LXII

Desgarrada la nube; el arco iris
brillando ya en el cielo,

y en un fanal de lluvia
y sol el campo envuelto.

Desperté. ¿Quién enturbia
los mágicos cristales de mi sueño?
Mi corazón latía
atónito y disperso.

... ¡El limonar florido,
el cipresal del huerto,
el prado verde, el sol, el agua, el iris ...
¡el agua en tus cabellos! ...

Y todo en la memoria se perdía
como una pompa de jabón al viento.

LXIII

Y era el demonio de mi sueño, el ángel
más hermoso. Brillaban
como aceros los ojos victoriosos,
y las sangrientas llamas
de su antorcha alumbraron
la honda cripta del alma.

—¿Vendrás conmigo? —No, jamás; las tumbas
y los muertos me espantan.
Pero la férrea mano
mi diestra atenazaba.

—Vendrás conmigo ... Y avancé en mi sueño
cegado por la roja luminaria.
Y en la cripta sentí sonar cadenas,
y rebullir de fieras enjauladas.

LXII

Tattered the cloud, the arching bow
radiant in the sky,

enveloped in screen of rain
and sun, the countryside.

I wakened then. Who befogged
the magic crystals of my dreaming?
Fearful and uncertain,
I found my heart was beating.

. . . Flowering lemon trees,
groves of cypress near,
meadow of green, sun, water, iris . . . ,
the raindrops on your hair!

And all within the memory lost
like a soap bubble blown on the air.

A. McV.

LXIII

And it was the demon of my dreams, most beautiful
of angels. A luminous glint
shone like steel in his victorious eyes
and blood-dripping flames were lit
as his torch shone round about
the soul's abysmal crypt.

"Will you come with me?" "No, never; tombs
and the dead are frightening."
But the grip of the iron hand
on mine was tightening.

"You will come with me . . ." And I went, in my dream,
blinded by redness blurring,
and in the crypt I sensed the rattling chains
and felt the terrible sound of caged beasts stirring.

A. McV.

117

LXIV

Desde el umbral de un sueño me llamaron . . .
Era la buena voz, la voz querida.

—Dime: ¿vendrás conmigo a ver el alma? . . .
Llegó a mi corazón una caricia.

—Contigo siempre . . . Y avancé en mi sueño
por una larga, escueta galería,
sintiendo el roce de la veste pura
y el palpitar suave de la mano amiga.

LXXII

La casa tan querida
donde habitaba ella,
sobre un montón de escombros arruinada
o derruída, enseña
el negro y carcomido
maltrabado esqueleto de madera.

La luna está vertiendo
su clara luz en sueños que platea
en las ventanas. Mal vestido y triste,
voy caminando por la calle vieja.

LXXIII

Ante el pálido lienzo de la tarde,
la iglesia, con sus torres afiladas
y el ancho campanario, en cuyos huecos
voltean suavemente las campanas,
alta y sombría, surge.

LXIV

From the threshold of a dream they called to me ...
It was the good voice, the voice of lovingness.

"Tell me: Will you come with me to see the soul? ..."
Into my heart there came then a caress.

"With you always ..." And I went, in my dream,
through a long, an empty corridor, and
I felt the contact of the innocent robe,
the softly throbbing pulse of a friendly hand.

A. McV.

LXXII

The house so dearly loved
where she once lived, became
a ruin, a wreck upon a rubbish heap,
blackened and decayed,
revealing now no more
than the worm-eaten skeleton of the wooden frame.

Tonight the moon is spilling
her brilliant argent light in dreams that sweep
silver on windows. Poorly dressed and sad,
I come to walk again through this old street.

A. McV.

LXXIII

Against the pale canvas of twilight
the church its tall sadness distills,
with needle-sharp towers outreaching
the squat campanile whose openings
reveal the smooth swinging of bells.

119

La estrella es una lágrima
en el azul celeste.
Bajo la estrella clara,
flota, vellón disperso,
una nube quimérica de plata.

LXXIV

Tarde tranquila, casi
con placidez de alma,
para ser joven, para haberlo sido
cuando Dios quiso, para
tener algunas alegrías ... lejos,
y poder dulcemente recordarlas.

LXXVI

¡Oh tarde luminosa!
El aire está encantado.
La blanca cigüeña,
dormita volando,
y las golondrinas se cruzan, tendidas
las alas agudas al viento dorado,
y en la tarde risueña se alejan
volando, soñando ...

Y hay una que torna como la saeta,
las alas agudas tendidas al aire sombrío,
buscando su negro rincón del tejado.

La blanca cigüeña,
como un garabato,
tranquila y disforme ¡tan disparatada!
sobre el campanario.

In the celestial blue of the heavens
the star is a teardrop in space,
and under its starry translucence
a cloud of chimerical silver
floats like a tatter of fleece.

J. R. L.

LXXIV

Tranquil evening, almost
with placid heart and bliss,
for being young, for having been so
while it was God's wish,
for certain joys that were known . . . once,
and for remembering tenderly all this.

A. McV.

LXXVI

O luminous afternoon!
Enchanted airs are sighing.
The white-winged stork
is drowsily flying
and swallows crisscross through the air,
sharp wings spread to gold winds streaming,
soaring off on a smiling day,
wheeling, dreaming . . .

And one there is that like an arrow swerves
to seek its own black corner of the roof,
stretched on shadowy air, sharp wings revealing.

The white-winged bird
like a scrawl on air,
tranquil, ill-formed—so absurd!—
over the belfry there.

A. McV.

LXXVII

Es una tarde cenicienta y mustia,
destartalada, como el alma mía;
y es esta vieja angustia
que habita mi usual hipocondría.

   La causa de esta angustia no consigo
ni vagamente comprender siquiera;
pero recuerdo y, recordando, digo:
—Sí, yo era niño, y tú, mi compañera.

*

   Y no es verdad, dolor, yo te conozco,
tú eres nostalgia de la vida buena
y soledad de corazón sombrío,
de barco sin naufragio y sin estrella.

   Como perro olvidado que no tiene
huella ni olfato y yerra
por los caminos, sin camino, como
el niño que en la noche de una fiesta

   se pierde entre el gentío
y el aire polvoriento y las candelas
chispeantes, atónito, y asombra
su corazón de música y de pena,

   así voy yo, borracho melancólico,
guitarrista lunático, poeta,
y pobre hombre en sueños,
siempre buscando a Dios entre la niebla.

LXXVII

On this evening, languid, ashen-gray,
gloomy and cluttered like my very heart,
this old grief comes to play
its wonted hypochondriac part.

I can assign no cause to this dismay,
having not the vaguest understanding,
but I remember, and remembering, say:
Yes, I was a boy and you were my companion.

*

No, grief, that is not true; I recognize
in you nostalgia for the good life lived,
the solitude that in a dark heart lies,
the yet unbattered, unwrecked, starless ship.

Like a forgotten dog that finds no path,
no scent, and goes astray,
following trails without a trail, or like
the child on festival night who has lost his way

among the thronging crowd,
air all dusty and the flares all sparkling,
terrified there amid the horde,
music and grief the young heart darkening;

thus go I, a lunatic guitarist,
poet in sad, inebriate daze,
and a man impoverished in his dreams,
forever seeking God amidst the haze.

A. McV.

LXXIX

Desnuda está la tierra,
y el alma aúlla al horizonte pálido
como loba famélica. ¿Qué buscas,
poeta, en el ocaso?

Amargo caminar, porque el camino
pesa en el corazón. ¡El viento helado,
y la noche que llega, y la amargura
de la distancia! . . . En el camino blanco

algunos yertos árboles negrean;
en los montes lejanos
hay oro y sangre . . . El sol murió . . . ¿Qué buscas,
poeta, en el ocaso?

LXXX
(CAMPO)

La tarde está muriendo
como un hogar humilde que se apaga.

Allá, sobre los montes,
quedan algunas brasas.

Y ese árbol roto en el camino blanco
hace llorar de lástima.

¡Dos ramas en el tronco herido, y una
hoja marchita y negra en cada rama!

¿Lloras? . . . Entre los álamos de oro,
lejos, la sombra del amor te aguarda.

124

LXXIX

Denuded is the land
and the soul is howling toward the pale horizon
like a famished she-wolf. What do you seek,
poet, in the west?

Bitter it is to walk because the road
weighs upon the heart. The icy wind,
night drawing near, and the bitterness
of distance ahead! There on the white road

are rigid trees merging into blackness;
on distant mountains—gold
and blood ... The sun has died ... What do you seek,
poet, in the west?

A. McV.

LXXX

COUNTRYSIDE

Now dies the afternoon
as on a humble hearth the fading flame.

There above the mountains
a few live coals remain.

That broken tree on the dust-white road
for pity makes one weep.

Two branches on a wounded trunk, and one
lone black and withered leaf on each.

You weep? Far off, the shadow of love
awaits you in the golden poplar trees.

A. McV.

125

LXXXV

La primavera besaba
suavemente la arboleda,
y el verde nuevo brotaba
como una verde humareda.

Las nubes iban pasando
sobre el campo juvenil . . .
Yo vi en las hojas temblando
las frescas lluvias de abril.

Bajo ese almendro florido,
todo cargado de flor,
—recordé—, yo he maldecido
mi juventud sin amor.

Hoy, en mitad de la vida,
me he parado a meditar . . .
¿Juventud nunca vivida,
quién te volviera a soñar?

LXXXVI

Eran ayer mis dolores
como gusanos de seda
que iban labrando capullos;
hoy son mariposas negras.

¡De cuántas flores amargas
he sacado blanca cera!
¡Oh, tiempo en que mis pesares
trabajaban como abejas!

Hoy son como avenas locas,
o cizaña en sementera,
como tizón en espiga,
como carcoma en madera.

LXXXV

Tenderly by spring
the grove of trees was kissed,
and green the buds appeared
like a veil of verdant mist.

Clouds were floating over
fields of sprouting grain . . .
Aquiver on leaves I saw
fresh drops of April rain.

Under a blossoming almond
where thick the flowers grew,
I remembered cursing
the loveless youth I knew.

Today, half way through life,
pondering I have been . . .
Youth I never lived,
who would dream you again?

A. M. M.

LXXXVI

As silkworms spin cocoons
my griefs of yesterday
spun theirs and are become
black butterflies today.

How many flowers were bitter,
yet wax I took from these!
Oh, days in which my troubles
labored like honeybees!

Now they are like the darnel,
wild oats that spoil the good,
blight upon the wheat,
or borers in the wood.

127

¡Oh, tiempo en que mis dolores
tenían lágrimas buenas,
y eran como agua de noria
que va regando una huerta!
Hoy son agua de torrente
que arranca el limo a la tierra.

Dolores que ayer hicieron
de mi corazón colmena,
hoy tratan mi corazón
como a una muralla vieja:
quieren derribarlo, y pronto,
al golpe de la piqueta.

X C

Los árboles conservan
verdes aún las copas,
pero del verde mustio
de las marchitas frondas.

El agua de la fuente,
sobre la piedra tosca
y de verdín cubierta,
resbala silenciosa.

Arrastra el viento algunas
amarillentas hojas.
¡El viento de la tarde
sobre la tierra en sombra!

Oh, time in which my sorrows
wept a healing flow,
like waters of a noria
making a garden grow!
Today, destructive torrents,
they ruin as they go.

Sorrows that made my heart
a hive that held them all
assail my heart today
like an old and crumbling wall,
wielding a heavy pickaxe,
wishing to see it fall.

H. E. F.

X C

The treetops still preserve
their covering of green,
but now the green is withered,
the green of fading leaves.

The water from the fountain
of roughly carven stone,
across the mold of ages
glides without a sound.

Crumpled yellow leaves
are dragged upon the wind.
The wind of afternoon
across the shadowed land.

J. R. L.

Húmedo está, bajo el laurel, el banco
de verdinosa piedra;
lavó la lluvia, sobre el muro blanco,
las empolvadas hojas de la hiedra.

Del viento del otoño el tibio aliento
los céspedes undula, y la alameda
conversa con el viento . . .
¡el viento de la tarde en la arboleda!

Mientras el sol en el ocaso esplende
que los racimos de la vid orea,
y el buen burgués, en su balcón, enciende
la estoica pipa en que el tabaco humea,

voy recordando versos juveniles . . .
¿Qué fué de aquel mi corazón sonoro?
¿Será cierto que os vais, sombras gentiles,
huyendo entre los árboles de oro?

XCVIII
(A ORILLAS DEL DUERO)

¡Oh, tierra triste y noble,
la de los altos llanos y yermos y roquedas,
de campos sin arados, regatos ni arboledas;
decrépitas ciudades, caminos sin mesones,
y atónitos palurdos sin danzas ni canciones
que aun van, abandonando el mortecino hogar,
como tus largos ríos, Castilla, hacia la mar!

XCI

Damp it is, under the laurel, the bench
of greenish-growing stone;
the rain came washing over the wall of white
until the dusty leaves of the ivy shone.

Warm the breath of autumn wind is blowing,
gently the grasses sway,
the poplars talk with the wind ...
on the grove of trees the wind of waning day!

While the sun in the western sky is casting splendor
and clusters on the grapevine turn to gold,
and the good bourgeois on his balcony has lit
his stoic pipe and smoke has upward rolled,

I go my way, recalling youthful verses ...
What happened to my heart, its melodies?
Is it true that you are gone, my graceful shadows,
fleeing from me through the golden trees?

                                                        A. McV.

XCVIII

ON THE BANKS OF THE DUERO

                        O sad and noble land
of high plains and wildernesses, wastes of rock,
of fields without plows, rivulets, or forest stock,
of roads without inns, of decrepit cities long decayed,
of bewildered rustics who neither dance nor song have made
for beauty, who leave the dying fires of home and flee,
like your long streams, Castilla, escaping to the sea.

Castilla miserable, ayer dominadora,
envuelta en sus andrajos desprecia cuanto ignora.
¿Espera, duerme o sueña? ¿La sangre derramada
recuerda, cuando tuvo la fiebre de la espada?
Todo se mueve, fluye, discurre, corre o gira;
cambian la mar y el monte y el ojo que los mira.
¿Pasó? Sobre sus campos aun el fantasma yerra
de un pueblo que ponía a Dios sobre la guerra.

La madre en otro tiempo fecunda en capitanes
madrastra es hoy apenas de humildes ganapanes.
Castilla no es aquella tan generosa un día,
cuando Myo Cid Rodrigo el de Vivar volvía,
ufano de su nueva fortuna y su opulencia,
a regalar a Alfonso los huertos de Valencia;
o que, tras la aventura que acreditó sus bríos,
pedía la conquista de los inmensos ríos
indianos a la corte, la madre de soldados,
guerreros y adalides que han de tornar, cargados
de plata y oro, a España, en regios galeones,
para la presa cuervos, para la lid leones.
Filósofos nutridos de sopa de convento
contemplan impasibles el amplio firmamento;
y si les llega en sueños, como un rumor distante,
clamor de mercaderes de muelles de Levante,
no acudirán siquiera a preguntar ¿qué pasa?
Y ya la guerra ha abierto las puertas de su casa.

Castilla miserable, ayer dominadora,
envuelta en sus harapos desprecia cuanto ignora.

(Lines 36-70)

XCIX
(POR TIERRAS DE ESPAÑA)

El hombre de estos campos que incendia los pinares
y su despojo aguarda como botín de guerra,
antaño hubo raído los negros encinares,
talado los robustos robledos de la sierra.

132

Miserable Castilla, once high over friend and foe,
in tatters wrapped, despises what she does not know.
Does she wait or sleep or dream? Remember the blood spilled
when her veins with the fever of the sword were filled?
Everything moves, flows, rambles, runs, or turns,
sea and mountain change and the eye that now discerns.
No longer? Over these fields there wanders as before
the ghost of a race that throned its God on strife and war.

Once captains were her sons, perennially renewed,
now all she has to mother is an alien brood
of lowly drudges; Castilla's gifts less generous are
than in the time My Cid Rodrigo de Bivar
returned, proud of his wealth, of fortunate new gains,
to make Valencian orchards now his sovereign's;
or when, after the adventure which her mettle tried,
she demanded of the Court to conquer all the wide
streams of the distant Indies; mother of soldiers brave,
of warriors and chieftains who would recross the wave
in regal galleons with gold and silver laden; scions,
eager crows for booty, for the battle, lions.
Philosophers who feed themselves on convent soup,
view without emotion the heaven's starry troop,
and if a distant rumor as in dreams they hear
of merchants shouting from a Catalonian pier,
they will not even turn to seek its cause, though war
sweeps through their house, opening every door.

Miserable Castilla, once queening friend and foe,
in tatters wrapped, despises what she does not know.

R. M. A.

XCIX
SPANISH COUNTRYSIDE

The man of these fields who burns the pine trees down,
yet hoards their fallen branches like the loot of war,
yesterday rooted up the black encina groves
and cut the sturdy oaks that once the mountain bore.

133

Hoy ve sus pobres hijos huyendo de sus lares;
la tempestad llevarse los limos de la tierra
por los sagrados ríos hacia los anchos mares;
y en páramos malditos trabaja, sufre y yerra.

Es hijo de una estirpe de rudos caminantes,
pastores que conducen sus hordas de merinos
a Extremadura fértil, rebaños trashumantes
que mancha el polvo y dora el sol de los caminos.

Pequeño, ágil, sufrido, los ojos de hombre astuto,
hundidos, recelosos, movibles; y trazadas
cual arco de ballesta, en el semblante enjuto
de pómulos salientes, las cejas muy pobladas.

Abunda el hombre malo del campo y de la aldea,
capaz de insanos vicios y crímenes bestiales,
que bajo el pardo sayo esconde un alma fea,
esclava de los siete pecados capitales.

Los ojos siempre turbios de envidia o de tristeza,
guarda su presa y llora la que el vecino alcanza;
ni para su infortunio ni goza su riqueza;
le hieren y acongojan fortuna y malandanza.

El numen de estos campos es sanguinario y fiero;
al declinar la tarde, sobre el remoto alcor,
veréis agigantarse la forma de un arquero,
la forma de un inmenso centauro flechador.

Veréis llanuras bélicas y páramos de asceta
—no fué por estos campos el bíblico jardín—;
son tierras para el águila, un trozo de planeta
por donde cruza errante la sombra de Caín.

Today his impoverished sons are fleeing from their homes,
tempestuous rains gnaw out the precious upper soils
carried by sacred rivers to swell the ample seas,
while in accursèd steppes he suffers, errs, and toils.

He is descended from a line of travelers rude,
shepherds who yearly drive their hordes of sheep upon
the road to rich Extremadura—nomadic flocks
stained by the highway dust and gilded by the sun.

He is agile, small, long-suffering; eyes of a man
astute flicker in caverns of the haggard face;
sunken, suspicious, they gleam above the jutting bones,
under the crossbow arch that the heavy eyebrows trace.

In field and village there is many an evil-hearted man
whom vices insane and bestial iniquities deprave;
under his gray-brown cloak an ugly soul is hid,
of the seven deadly sins the gross and willing slave.

His eyes are always clouded with envy or with grief,
he keeps his prey and mourns that won by any neighbor;
from happy fate or ill he draws the selfsame wound—
he neither fends misfortune nor enjoys the fruit of labor.

The spirit of these fields is a bloody one and proud,
and when the day declines upon the distant hill
you will see mount high and higher a giant archer's form,
Sagittarius with his arrow aiming for the kill.

Ascetic steppes you'll see and prairies racked with war—
Eden never flourished on this treeless plain—
it was fashioned for the eagle, a piece of planet where
still unquiet wanders the sombre shade of Cain.

                                        R. M. A.

CI
(EL DIOS IBERO)

Igual que el ballestero
tahur de la cantiga,
tuviera una saeta el hombre ibero
para el Señor que apedreó la espiga
y malogró los frutos otoñales,
y un "gloria a ti" para el Señor que grana
centenos y trigales
que el pan bendito le darán mañana.

"Señor de la ruina,
adoro porque aguardo y porque temo:
con mi oración se inclina
hacia la tierra un corazón blasfemo.

¡Señor, por quien arranco el pan con pena,
sé tu poder, conozco mi cadena!
¡Oh dueño de la nube del estío
que la campiña arrasa,
del seco otoño, del helar tardío
y del bochorno que la mies abrasa!

¡Señor del iris, sobre el campo verde
donde la oveja pace,
Señor del fruto que el gusano muerde
y de la choza que el turbión deshace,

tu soplo el fuego del hogar aviva,
tu lumbre da sazón al rubio grano,
y cuaja el hueso de la verde oliva,
la noche de San Juan, tu santa mano!

¡Oh dueño de fortuna y de pobreza,
ventura y malandanza,
que al rico das favores y pereza
y al pobre su fatiga y su esperanza!

136

CI
IBERIAN GOD

As the gambler drew his bow
for vengeance in the song,
so the Iberian recklessly let go
a sharp shaft to the Lord of blighting wrong
who felled his wheat with hail and killed his fruit;
but he praised the Lord who brought his crops to head
full eared, gold to the root,
the rye and wheat that tomorrow would be his bread.

"Lord of ruin and loss,
I adore because I fear, because I wait,
but my heart is blasphemous:
bowing to earth, I pray in pride and hate.

"I know Thy power, my chain I recognize,
Lord, for Thee I dig my bread in sweat and sighs;
O master of the flooding clouds that cost
so dear to summer yield,
of the autumn drought and spring's belated frost,
of the scorching heat that sears the harvest field.

"Lord of the bow above the tender grass
where the white ewe grazes,
Lord of the hut undone when tempests pass
and of the fruit where the worm carves its mazes,

"Thy breathing quickens the hearth fire when it
is low, Thy splendor ripens ruddy grain,
and on Midsummer Eve the olive pit
forms and hardens where Thy hand has lain.

"O master of fortunes and of poverties,
good luck and bad, who yet
giv'st to the rich man favors and soft ease
and to the poor, his hope and bitter sweat.

¡Señor, Señor: en la voltaria rueda
del año he visto mi simiente echada,
corriendo igual albur que la moneda
del jugador en el azar sembrada!

¡Señor, hoy paternal, ayer cruento,
con doble faz de amor y de venganza,
a ti, en un dado de tahur al viento
va mi oración, blasfemia y alabanza!"

Este que insulta a Dios en los altares,
no más atento al ceño del destino,
también soñó caminos en los mares
y dijo: es Dios sobre la mar camino.

¿No es él quien puso a Dios sobre la guerra,
más allá de la suerte,
más allá de la tierra,
más allá de la mar y de la muerte?

¿No dió la encina ibera
para el fuego de Dios la buena rama,
que fué en la santa hoguera
de amor una con Dios en pura llama?

Mas hoy . . . ¡Qué importa un día!
Para los nuevos lares
estepas hay en la floresta umbría,
leña verde en los viejos encinares.

Aun larga patria espera
abrir al corvo arado sus besanas;
para el grano de Dios hay sementera
bajo cardos y abrojos y bardanas.

¡Que importa un día! Está el ayer alerto
al mañana, mañana al infinito,
hombres de España, ni el pasado ha muerto,
ni está el mañana—ni el ayer—escrito.

138

"Lord, Lord, in the twelve months' whirling round
I have watched my seed with patient labor sown
run the same risk in the hard and faithless ground
as a gambler's cash on the losing hazard thrown.

"Lord, paternal now, who wert before a God
cruel, two-faced, Thy love with vengeance dimmed,
to Thee my prayer of blasphemy and laud
ascends, a gambler's die cast on the wind."

This man who, insulting God, at His altar prayed,
defiant of all fate's frowning might forbode,
with dreaming tamed the seas and highways laid
across them, saying, He is the ocean road.

Is it not this man who raised his God to be
above all war? Beyond
fate, beyond earth and sea,
beyond death and dying, free of every bond?

Did not the Iberian tree,
the encina, yield her branch for holy fire
and, burning, find unity
with God in love's pure flame on the sacred pyre?

But now, so quickly day grows into day!
There are new hearths; for these
new roses thrive in field and wooded bay
and fresh green branches on the ancient trees.

The fatherland is still
waiting to open furrows to the plow;
for the seed of God there is a field to till,
overgrown with burdocks, thorns and thistles now.

Day merges into day; the past is wide
to the morrow, the morrow to the infinite;
men of Spain, no yesterday has died,
future and past have yet no holy writ.

139

¿Quién ha visto la faz al Dios hispano?
Mi corazón aguarda
al hombre ibero de la recia mano,
que tallará en el roble castellano
el Dios adusto de la tierra parda.

C V
(EN ABRIL, LAS AGUAS MIL)

Son de abril las aguas mil.
Sopla el viento achubascado,
y entre nublado y nublado
hay trozos de cielo añil.

Agua y sol. El iris brilla.
En una nube lejana,
zigzaguea
una centella amarilla.

La lluvia da en la ventana
y el cristal repiquetea.

A través de la neblina
que forma la lluvia fina,
se divisa un prado verde,
y un encinar se esfumina,
y una sierra gris se pierde.

Los hilos del aguacero
sesgan las nacientes frondas,
y agitan las turbias ondas
en el remanso del Duero.

Lloviendo está en los habares
y en las pardas sementeras;
hay sol en los encinares,
charcos por las carreteras.

Did ever the Spanish God His face reveal?
My heart awaits the hand
of an Iberian, vigorous and leal,
to carve in oaken timbers of Castile
the God austere who reigns in this brown land.

R. M. A.

C V

APRIL CONTAINS A THOUSAND RAINS

April contains a thousand rains.
The wind-borne squalls blow high
and fragments of indigo sky
through cloud and cloud show plain.

Water and sun. A rainbow's arc.
In a distant cloud
a zigzagging flame
cuts yellow through dark.

The window is rattling loud
under the pounding rain.

Clear through the delicate mist
of the fine rain's synthesis,
a meadow of green is discerned,
but a gray sierra is lost
and to shadow an oak is turned.

Aqueous filaments bend
the tender, nascent blades
and stir to turbulent waves
the quietness of the Duero.

It is raining on fields of beans,
raining where lands are sown;
sunlight falls on oak trees,
pools mark wagon roads.

Lluvia y sol. Ya se obscurece
el campo, ya se ilumina;
allí un cerro desparece,
allá surge una colina.

Ya son claros, ya sombríos
los dispersos caseríos,
los lejanos torreones.

Hacia la sierra plomiza
van rodando en pelotones
nubes de guata y ceniza.

CIX
(AMANECER DE OTOÑO)

A Julio Romero de Torres.

Una larga carretera
entre grises peñascales,
y alguna humilde pradera
donde pacen negros toros. Zarzas, malezas, jarales.

Está la tierra mojada
por las gotas del rocío,
y la alameda dorada,
hacia la curva del río.

Tras los montes de violeta
quebrado el primer albor;
a la espalda la escopeta,
entre sus galgos agudos, caminando un cazador.

Rain and sun. The fields, unclear,
resolve from dark to light;
here a knoll disappears,
there one emerges to sight.

First sun, then cloud, encases
the scattered country places
and distant battle towers.

Toward leaden peaks now lifting
platoons of cotton tufts
and ashen clouds are drifting.

A. McV.

CIX

AUTUMN DAWN

To Julio Romero de Torres

A highroad's barren scar
among the gray rock-spires,
and humble pastures far
where strong black bulls are grazing. Brambles, thickets, briars.

The dew has drenched with cold
the landscape in the dark
and the poplars' frieze of gold,
toward the river's arc.

A hint of dawn half seen
with purple crags for frame.
Beside his greyhounds keen,
his eager gun at rest, a hunter stalking game.

J. R. L.

CXI

(NOCHE DE VERANO)

Es una hermosa noche de verano.
Tienen las altas casas
abiertos los balcones
del viejo pueblo a la anchurosa plaza.
En el amplio rectángulo desierto,
bancos de piedra, evónimos y acacias
simétricos dibujan
sus negras sombras en la arena blanca.
En el cenit, la luna, y en la torre,
la esfera del reloj iluminada.
Yo en este viejo pueblo paseando
solo, como un fantasma.

CXII

(PASCUA DE RESURRECCIÓN)

Mirad: el arco de la vida traza
el iris sobre el campo que verdea.
Buscad vuestros amores, doncellitas,
donde brota la fuente de la piedra.
En donde el agua ríe y sueña y pasa,
allí el romance del amor se cuenta.
¿No han de mirar un día, en vuestros brazos,
atónitos, el sol de primavera,
ojos que vienen a la luz cerrados,
y que al partirse de la vida ciegan?
¿No beberán un día en vuestros senos
los que mañana labrarán la tierra?
¡Oh, celebrad este domingo claro,
madrecitas en flor, vuestras entrañas nuevas!
Gozad esta sonrisa de vuestra ruda madre.
Ya sus hermosos nidos habitan las cigüeñas,
y escriben en las torres sus blancos garabatos.
Como esmeraldas lucen los musgos de las peñas.
Entre los robles muerden
los negros toros la menuda hierba,
y el pastor que apacienta los merinos
su pardo sayo en la montaña deja.

CXI

SUMMER NIGHT

It is a beautiful summer night.
There in the tall houses
the open balconies
of the old town face the ample plaza.
In the spacious, deserted rectangle,
benches of stone, symmetrical trees—
spindles and locusts—
sketch their own black shadows on white sand.
In its zenith, the moon, and in the tower
the sphere of the lighted clock.
And I, walking this old town
alone, like a ghost.

A. McV.

CXII

EASTER

Look: over the greening countryside
the arc of life follows the iris' bow.
Go in search, young maidens, of your loves
where waters from the stone-hewn fountain flow.
Wherever water laughs and dreams and runs
there will the old romance of love unfold.
Will not a creature in your arms one day
with startled eyes the sun of spring behold,
eyes that are closed in greeting to the world
and blindly turn from it again to go?
Is it not at your young breasts that they will drink
who tomorrow will strive the hard land to subdue?
Oh, celebrate in the brightness of this Sunday,
young mothers in flower, new mysteries within you.
Revel in the infrequent smile that comes from your stern mother.
Once more the storks are dwelling in their beautiful nests,
writing their white scrawls again upon the towers.
Like emeralds gleam the mosses of the rocks.
On shoots of tender green
the black bulls graze among the mighty oaks
and the shepherd watching patiently his sheep
leaves on the mountainside his heavy cloak.

A. McV.

145

CXIII

(CAMPOS DE SORIA)

VI

¡Soria fría, *Soria pura,*
cabeza de Extremadura,
con su castillo guerrero
arruinado, sobre el Duero;
con sus murallas roídas
y sus casas denegridas!

¡Muerta ciudad de señores
soldados o cazadores;
de portales con escudos
de cien linajes hidalgos,
y de famélicos galgos,
de galgos flacos y agudos,
que pululan
por las sórdidas callejas,
y a la media noche ululan,
cuando graznan las cornejas!

¡Soria fría! La campana
de la Audiencia da la una.
Soria, ciudad castellana
¡tan bella! bajo la luna.

VIII

He vuelto a ver los álamos dorados,
álamos del camino en la ribera
del Duero, entre San Polo y San Saturio,
tras las murallas viejas
de Soria—barbacana
hacia Aragón, en castellana tierra.

CXIII
FIELDS OF SORIA

VI

Soria cold, Soria pure,
stronghold of Extremadura,
whose warrior castle stands
ruined on Duero's banks;
time-stained houses in the town
and old walls falling down.

Dead city of proud race
who follow war or the chase;
of doors where coats of arms
of ancestors abound,
and packs of starveling hounds
in lean and hungry swarms
that roam and prowl
through each sordid, dingy lane
and then at midnight howl
when the cawing crows complain!

Soria cold! The bell
of the city hall strikes one.
Soria, city of Castile,
how fair beneath the moon!

VIII

I have come back to see the golden poplars,
poplars by the road along the bank
of the Duero, between San Polo and San Saturio,
beyond the ancient walls that stand
round Soria—a bulwark
towards Aragón, within Castilian land.

Estos chopos del río, que acompañan
con el sonido de sus hojas secas
el son del agua, cuando el viento sopla,
tienen en sus cortezas
grabadas iniciales que son nombres
de enamorados, cifras que son fechas.
¡Alamos del amor que ayer tuvisteis
de ruiseñores vuestras ramas llenas;
álamos que seréis mañana liras
del viento perfumado en primavera;
álamos del amor cerca del agua
que corre y pasa y sueña,
álamos de las márgenes del Duero,
conmigo vais, mi corazón os lleva!

CXVI
(RECUERDOS)

¡Oh Soria, cuando miro los frescos naranjales
cargados de perfume, y el campo enverdecido,
abiertos los jazmines, maduros los trigales,
azules las montañas y el olivar florido;
Guadalquivir corriendo al mar entre vergeles;
y al sol de abril los huertos colmados de azucenas,
y los enjambres de oro, para libar sus mieles
dispersos en los campos, huir de sus colmenas;
yo sé la encina roja crujiendo en tus hogares,
barriendo el cierzo helado tu campo empedernido;
y en sierras agrias sueño—¡Urbión, sobre pinares!
¡Moncayo blanco, al cielo aragonés, erguido!—
Y pienso: Primavera, como un escalofrío
irá a cruzar el alto solar del romancero,
ya verdearán los chopos las márgenes del río.
¿Dará sus verdes hojas el olmo aquel del Duero?
Tendrán los campanarios de Soria sus cigüeñas,
y la roqueda parda más de un zarzar en flor;
ya los rebaños blancos, por entre grises peñas,
hacia los altos prados conducirá el pastor.

These aspens by the river growing,
that accompany with the rustle of dry leaves
the sound of water when the wind is blowing,
have initials that are names
of lovers in their bark engraved,
numbers that are dates.
Poplars of love that yesterday
had branches full of nightingales to sing;
poplars that tomorrow will be lyres
for the perfumed wind of spring;
poplars of love beside the waters
that run and dream and flow,
poplars on the Duero riverbanks,
I carry you in my heart; with me you go!

B. G. P.

CXVI

MEMORIES

O Soria, when I see the freshness of orange groves,
heavy with their perfume, and the greening field,
jasmines opening now, the wheat stalks ripening,
azure of the mountains, olive grove in bloom,
the Guadalquivir running through flowers to the sea,
and under the sun of April, gardens rife with lilies
while swarms of golden bees are fleeing from their hives,
questing far for honey to sip in the open fields,
I know how the red encina is crackling on your hearths
and how the frozen wind sweeps your indurate ground;
as I dream of harsh sierras—Urbión above the pines,
Moncayo white against the sky of Aragón!—
I am thinking, Spring, how like a chill you'll be
when you go up to cross the *romancero* highlands;
green will grow the poplars on the river banks.
And that elm beside the Duero, will it sprout verdant leaves?
Then shall Sorian bell towers receive their storks again,
and, amid gray rocks, more than one thicket will bloom.
Through a stony way will the shepherd lead white flocks
between the gray boulders to grasslands on the heights.

¡Oh, en el azul, vosotras, viajeras golondrinas
que vais al joven Duero, rebaños de merinos,
con rumbo hacia las altas praderas numantinas,
por las cañadas hondas y al sol de los caminos;
hayedos y pinares que cruza el ágil ciervo,
montañas, serrijones, lomazos, parameras,
en donde reina el águila, por donde busca el cuervo
su infecto expoliario; menudas sementeras
cual sayos cenicientos, casetas y majadas
entre desnuda roca, arroyos y hontanares
donde a la tarde beben las yuntas fatigadas,
dispersos huertecillos, humildes abejares! . . .

¡Adiós, tierra de Soria; adiós el alto llano
cercado de colinas y crestas militares,
alcores y roquedas del yermo castellano,
fantasmas de robledos y sombras de encinares!

En la desesperanza y en la melancolía
de tu recuerdo, Soria, mi corazón se abreva.
Tierra de alma, toda, hacia la tierra mía,
por los floridos valles, mi corazón te lleva.

En el tren.—abril 1912.

CXIX

Señor, ya me arrancaste lo que yo más quería.
Oye otra vez, Dios mío, mi corazón clamar.
Tu voluntad se hizo, Señor, contra la mía.
Señor, ya estamos solos mi corazón y el mar.

Oh, up into blueness will you go, wandering swallows,
toward the young Duero and flocks of merino sheep
making their way upward to high Numantian prairies,
traveling deep-cut canyons under the sun of the roads;
to forest of beech and pine, crossed by the agile deer,
to mountains, ridged sierras, hillocks and arid places
where the eagle reigns, where the crow is seeking
tainted spoil; to the little plots of seeded land
spread out like ashen garments; cottages and sheep-cots
amid the barren rocks, to streams and generous springs
where the weary beasts drink at eventide,
to tiny scattered gardens and crudely made beehives.

Farewell, land of Soria, farewell to the lofty plain
enclosed and ringed about by heights and warlike crests,
to the hills and to the rock-strewn lands of bare Castile,
ghosts of sylvan oaks and shades of olive groves.

Here in my despair, here in my melancholy,
Soria, is my heart refreshed by your memory.
Land of the soul, my land, all of this my heart
through the flowering valleys carries back to you.

On the train—April 1912

A. McV.

CXIX

Lord, Thou hast taken what I held most dear.
Hear once more, my God, my heart's threnody.
Thy will was done, O Lord, not mine.
Lord, we are alone, my heart and the sea.

A. McV.

CXX

Dice la esperanza: un día
la verás, si bien esperas.
Dice la desesperanza:
sólo tu amargura es ella.
Late, corazón... No todo
se lo ha tragado la tierra.

CXXI

Allá, en las tierras altas
por donde traza el Duero
su curva de ballesta
en torno a Soria, entre plomizos cerros
y manchas de raídos encinares,
mi corazón está vagando, en sueños...

¿No ves, Leonor, los álamos del río
con sus ramajes yertos?
Mira el Moncayo azul y blanco; dame
tu mano y paseemos.
Por estos campos de la tierra mía,
bordados de olivares polvorientos,
voy caminando solo,
triste, cansado, pensativo y viejo.

CXXIII

Una noche de verano
—estaba abierto el balcón
y la puerta de mi casa—
la muerte en mi casa entró.
Se fué acercando a su lecho
—ni siquiera me miró—,
con unos dedos muy finos,
algo muy tenue rompió.
Silenciosa y sin mirarme,
la muerte otra vez pasó
delante de mí. ¿Qué has hecho?
La muerte no respondió.

CXX

Hope says: "You shall see her
one day if hope endures."
Despair: "Your bitterness
is all there is of her."
Beat, heart . . . Earth did not
swallow everything of yours.

A. McV.

CXXI

Up there in the highlands
where traces Duero's stream
its flex of a crossbow arch
round Soria; among the leaden peaks
and passing clusters of frayed encina groves,
wandering goes my heart, in its dreams.

See, Leonor, the poplars by the river,
their branches rigid poles?
Look at Moncayo, blue and white; give me
your hand and let us stroll.
Through the fields of this land that is my own,
these fields embroidered with dusty olive groves,
alone do I go walking,
weary, sad, pensive now, and old.

A. McV.

CXXIII

My balcony, one summer night,
was open to the air,
—the door was open in my house—
and Death found entrance there.
He came up close beside her bed
—nor gave a glance at me—
and broke with fingers very thin
a thing too fine to see.
Without a sound, without a glance,
again Death passed me by.
"What is it you have done?" I asked,
but Death made no reply.

153

Mi niña quedó tranquila,
dolido mi corazón.
¡Ay, lo que la muerte ha roto
era un hilo entre los dos!

CXXIV

Al borrarse la nieve, se alejaron
los montes de la sierra.
La vega ha verdecido
al sol de abril, la vega
tiene la verde llama,
la vida, que no pesa;
y piensa el alma en una mariposa,
atlas del mundo, y sueña.
Con el ciruelo en flor y el campo verde,
con el glauco vapor de la ribera,
en torno de las ramas,
con las primeras zarzas que blanquean,
con este dulce soplo
que triunfa de la muerte y de la piedra,
esta amargura que me ahoga fluye
en esperanza de Ella...

CXXV

En estos campos de la tierra mía,
y extranjero en los campos de mi tierra
—yo tuve patria donde corre el Duero
por entre grises peñas,
y fantasmas de viejos encinares,
allá en Castilla, mística y guerrera,
Castilla la gentil, humilde y brava,
Castilla del desdén y de la fuerza—,
en estos campos de mi Andalucía,
¡oh, tierra en que nací!, cantar quisiera.
Tengo recuerdos de mi infancia, tengo
imágenes de luz y de palmeras,
y en una gloria de oro,

In quiet sleep my love still lay,
my heart was filled with rue.
Alas, what Death had broken was
a tie between the two!

H. E. F.

CXXIV

The mountains have receded
with the vanishing of snow.
Under the sun of April
now green the prairies grow,
afire with gossamer life,
they burn a flame of green;
to a butterfly, world's atlas,
the heart has turned to dream.
With cherry in flower, field in verdure,
and river mist to brighten
the vaporous greening trees,
with the first of the brambles to whiten
and with this dulcet breeze,
of death and stone the vanquisher,
my drowning bitterness flows away
high in hopes of Her.

A. McV.

CXXV

Here within the fields of this land of mine,
and a stranger I within the fields of my land
(for I chose my country where the Duero flows
and gray the rock forms stand
'mid ghosts of old encinas,
Castile of mystic and warlike strain,
Castile the elegant, humble and brave,
Castile of strength and of disdain),
here in the fields of my Andalucía,
O land wherein I was born, thee I would sing.
Visions of light and groves of palms
memories of my childhood bring
and, in a glory of gold,

de lueñes campanarios con cigüeñas,
de ciudades con calles sin mujeres
bajo un cielo de añil, plazas desiertas
donde crecen naranjos encendidos
con sus frutas redondas y bermejas;
y en un huerto sombrío, el limonero
de ramas polvorientas
y pálidos limones amarillos,
que el agua clara de la fuente espeja,
un aroma de nardos y claveles
y un fuerte olor de albahaca y hierbabuena;
imágenes de grises olivares
bajo un tórrido sol que aturde y ciega,
y azules y dispersas serranías
con arreboles de una tarde inmensa;
mas falta el hilo que el recuerdo anuda
al corazón, el ancla en su ribera,
o estas memorias no son alma. Tienen,
en sus abigarradas vestimentas,
señal de ser despojos del recuerdo,
la carga bruta que el recuerdo lleva.
Un día tornarán, con luz del fondo ungidos,
los cuerpos virginales a la orilla vieja.

Lora del Río, 4 abril 1913.

CXXVI
(A JOSÉ MARÍA PALACIO)

Palacio, buen amigo,
¿está la primavera
vistiendo ya las ramas de los chopos
del río y los caminos? En la estepa
del alto Duero, Primavera tarda,
¡pero es tan bella y dulce cuando llega! ...
¿Tienen los viejos olmos
algunas hojas nuevas?
Aun las acacias estarán desnudas
y nevados los montes de las sierras.

far towers where the white storks fly,
cities whose streets are womanless,
their plazas deserted beneath an indigo sky,
and in the plazas, flaming orange trees
their rounded, ruddy-tinted fruit display,
and the lemon tree deep in a shady garden,
branches of dusty gray;
the pallid yellow lemons
within the bright, mirrorlike fountain glint;
aromas of spikenard, carnations,
and the pungent fragrance of basil and peppermint;
visions of gray olive groves
under a dizzying, blinding, tropical blaze
and scattered blue mountains, red-skied
through the endless afternoon of the days;
but there lacks the thread knotting memory to heart,
there lacks the anchor in its cove,
or the visions are not the heart itself. For they,
in their motley garments clothed,
wear the mark of memory's castoffs,
of the heavy burden recalling bears.
Yet one day will their virginal selves, in a shining light,
return again to the shores that once were theirs.

Lora del Río, April 4, 1913
A. McV.

CXXVI
TO JOSÉ MARÍA PALACIO

Palacio, good friend
has spring returned again,
clothing the branches of the poplars now
along the roads and river? Upon the high
lands of the Duero spring comes late
but when it comes how fair and sweet it is!
Have the old elms put out
some tentative new leaves?
The acacia trees will probably be bare
and snow will lie upon the mountain tops.

¡Oh, mole del Moncayo blanca y rosa,
allá, en el cielo de Aragón, tan bella!
¿Hay zarzas florecidas
entre las grises peñas,
y blancas margaritas
entre la fina hierba?
Por esos campanarios
ya habrán ido llegando las cigüeñas.
Habrá trigales verdes,
y mulas pardas en las sementeras,
y labriegos que siembran los tardíos
con las lluvias de abril. Ya las abejas
libarán del tomillo y el romero.
¿Hay ciruelos en flor? ¿Quedan violetas?
Furtivos cazadores, los reclamos
de la perdiz bajo las capas luengas,
no faltarán. Palacio, buen amigo,
¿tienen ya ruiseñores las riberas?
Con los primeros lirios
y las primeras rosas de las huertas,
en una tarde azul, sube al Espino,
al alto Espino donde está su tierra . . .

Baeza, 29 de abril 1913.

CXXIX

(NOVIEMBRE 1913)

Un año más. El sembrador va echando
la semilla en los surcos de la tierra.
Dos lentas yuntas aran,
mientras pasan las nubes cenicientas
ensombreciendo el campo,
las pardas sementeras,
los grises olivares. Por el fondo
del valle el río el agua turbia lleva.
Tiene Cazorla nieve,
y Mágina, tormenta,
su montera, Aznaitín. Hacia Granada,
montes con sol, montes de sol y piedra.

Oh, peak of Moncayo rose and white,
how lovely against the sky of Aragón!
Are the brambles yet in flower
among the gray of cliffs?
And are there daisies blooming
amid the tender grass?
Storks will have come
to nest upon the towers.
There will be green of wheat
and dun mules working in the fresh-plowed fields
and laborers who sow the waning day
with drops of April rain. And the bees
will be sipping now from thyme and rosemary.
Are the cherry trees in bloom? Are there violets still?
Furtive hunters in long capes
with partridge lures beneath
will not be lacking. Palacio, good friend,
have the riverbanks their nightingales so soon?
With the earliest of the lilies
and the earliest of roses in the gardens
in the blue twilight, go up to the Espino,
the high Espino, where her country is.

Baeza, April 29, 1913
B. G. P.

CXXIX

NOVEMBER 1913

Another year. The sower is tossing
the seed into furrowed soil.
Two slow yokes of oxen plowing,
while ashen clouds are passing,
shadowing the field,
the bare brown seeded land,
gray olive groves. Through the valley
the river carries its earth-stained water.
Cazorla has snow
and Mágina storms,
Aznaitín, its cap. And toward Granada,
mountains with sun, mountains of sun and stone.

J. R. L.

159

CXXX
(LA SAETA)

¿Quién me presta una escalera,
para subir al madero,
para quitarle los clavos
a Jesús el Nazareno?

Saeta popular

¡Oh, la saeta, el cantar
al Cristo de los gitanos,
siempre con sangre en las manos,
siempre por desenclavar!
¡Cantar del pueblo andaluz,
que todas las primaveras
anda pidiendo escaleras
para subir a la cruz!
¡Cantar de la tierra mía,
que echa flores
al Jesús de la agonía,
y es la fe de mis mayores!
¡Oh, no eres tú mi cantar!
¡No puedo cantar, ni quiero
a ese Jesús del madero,
sino al que anduvo en el mar!

CXXXII
(LOS OLIVOS)
A Manolo Ayuso.

I

¡Viejos olivos sedientos
bajo el claro sol del día,
olivares polvorientos
del campo de Andalucía!
¡El campo andaluz, peinado
por el sol canicular,
de loma en loma rayado
de olivar y de olivar!

160

CXXX
THE *SAETA*

Who will lend me a ladder
that I may climb to the beam
and take out the driven spikes
from Jesus the Nazarene?

Popular *saeta*

Oh, *saeta* of the gypsies' Christ,
song of the gypsy bands!
Always with blood on His hands,
always to draw out the spikes!
Andaluz words in rhyme,
every spring, in sorrow,
asking a ladder to borrow,
up to the cross they would climb.
Song of my native region,
flowers are tossed
to Jesus on the cross,
and this my elders' religion!
My faith you never shall be!
No song nor love I could
give to that Jesus on the rood,
but to Him who walked on the sea.

A. McV.

CXXXII
THE OLIVE TREES
To Manolo Ayuso

I

Olive trees old and thirsty
in sunlight, stand on stand,
dusty groves of olives
on Andalusian land.
Andaluz countryside,
by white sunlight combed,
striped from hill to hill
with grove on olive grove.

161

Son las tierras
soleadas,
anchas lomas, lueñes sierras
de olivares recamadas!
Mil senderos. Con sus machos,
abrumados de capachos,
van gañanes y arrieros.
De la venta del camino
a la puerta, soplan vino
trabucaires bandoleros!
Olivares y olivares
de loma en loma prendidos
cual bordados alamares!
Olivares coloridos
de una tarde anaranjada;
olivares rebruñidos
bajo la luna argentada!
Olivares centellados
en las tardes cenicientas,
bajo los cielos preñados
de tormentas! ...
Olivares, Dios os dé
los eneros
de aguaceros,
los agostos de agua al pie,
los vientos primaverales
vuestras flores racimadas;
y las lluvias otoñales,
vuestras olivas moradas.
Olivar, por cien caminos,
tus olivitas irán
caminando a cien molinos.
Ya darán
trabajo en las alquerías
a gañanes y braceros,
¡oh buenas frentes sombrías
bajo los anchos sombreros! ...
Olivar y olivareros,
bosque y raza,
campo y plaza

These are lands
of sunburned tones,
ample slopes and far sierras
embroidered with olive groves.
A thousand paths. Walking each
go the hamper-laden beasts
and workmen and drivers manifold.
From roadside mart, a different kind
approach the gate, exhaling wine,
thieving highwaymen bold!
From hill to hill displayed,
grove on olive grove
like swirls of embroidered braid!
Colorful olive trees
on an orange afternoon,
burnished bright again
under the silver moon!
Sparkling olive trees
on days ash-gray and warm
beneath the gravid skies
bearing storms . . .
O trees, these came from God:
January hours
of sudden showers,
Augusts of rain-wet sod;
from winds of early spring
your clustered blossoms came;
the purple fruit you bear,
from the autumnal rain.
Along a hundred paths
will the fruit of your branches wind,
bound for a hundred mills.
Farmers will find
work for eager hands
of all the laboring men.
Oh, under the wide-brimmed hats
the good, shadowed brows again!
Groves and working men,
woods and lineage,
field and village

163

de los fieles al terruño
y al arado y al molino,
de los que muestran el puño
al destino,
los benditos labradores,
los bandidos caballeros,
los señores
devotos y matuteros! . . .
Ciudades y caseríos
en la margen de los ríos,
en los pliegues de la sierra! . . .
Venga Dios a los hogares
y a las almas de esta tierra
de olivares y olivares!

CXXXVI
(PROVERBIOS Y CANTARES)

I

Nunca perseguí la gloria
ni dejar en la memoria
de los hombres mi canción;
yo amo los mundos sutiles,
ingrávidos y gentiles
como pompas de jabón.
Me gusta verlos pintarse
de sol y grana, volar
bajo el cielo azul, temblar
súbitamente y quebrarse.

XV

Cantad conmigo en coro: Saber, nada sabemos,
de arcano mar vinimos, a ignota mar iremos . . .
Y entre los dos misterios está el enigma grave;
tres arcas cierra una desconocida llave.
La luz nada ilumina y el sabio nada enseña.
¿Qué dice la palabra? ¿Qué el agua de la peña?

of those granting land and plow
and press fidelity
and of those who clench a fist
at destiny,
the blessed laborers,
the gentleman-bandits,
the highly born
devotee-contrabandists.
Cities and country towns
in mountain folds tucked down
or perched on river banks . . .
May God bless every home
and heart of this wooded land
of grove on olive grove.

A. McV.

CXXXVI

PROVERBS AND SONGS

I

No glory hunter have I been
nor one who would in minds of men
leave a song that is mine alone.
I love those worlds intangible,
infecund and frangible
as soap bubbles blown.
I like to see the gaudy spheres,
sun-dappled, scarlet-tinted, fly
under the blueness of the sky,
then suddenly burst and disappear.

XV

Chant with me in a chorus: To know, nothing we know,
from arcane sea we came, to unknown sea we go . . .
Between both mysteries will the enigma be;
three the coffers locked by an undiscovered key.
Light illumines nothing, the sage teaches naught.
What does the word say? And the water of the rock?

165

XXI

Ayer soñé que veía
a Dios y que a Dios hablaba;
y soñé que Dios me oía ...
Después soñé que soñaba.

XLIV

Todo pasa y todo queda;
pero lo nuestro es pasar,
pasar haciendo caminos,
caminos sobre la mar.

XLVI

Anoche soñé que oía
a Dios, gritándome: ¡Alerta!
Luego era Dios quien dormía,
y yo gritaba: ¡Despierta!

XLVII

Cuatro cosas tiene el hombre
que no sirven en la mar:
ancla, gobernalle y remos,
y miedo de naufragar.

CXXXVII
(PARÁBOLAS)

III

Erase de un marinero
que hizo un jardín junto al mar,
y se metió a jardinero.
Estaba el jardín en flor,
y el jardinero se fué
por esos mares de Dios.

Last night I dreamed that I saw
God, to whom I was speaking;
I dreamed that He listened to me ...
And later, dreamed I was dreaming.

XLIV

All passes and all stays;
to go is our decree,
to go opening roads,
pathways over the sea.

XLVI

I dreamed that I heard: "On guard!"
And it was God who spake.
Then it was God who slept
while I cried out: "Awake!"

XLVII

Four are the useless things
a man in the sea has found:
anchor, rudder, oars,
and fear of being drowned.

A. McV.

CXXXVII

PARABLES

III

Was a sailor left the sea
and made a garden near;
a gardener he would be.
In bloom were the orchard trees,
and the gardener went away
to sail upon God's seas.

B. G. P.

VI

El Dios que todos llevamos,
el Dios que todos hacemos,
el Dios que todos buscamos
y que nunca encontraremos.
Tres dioses o tres personas
del solo Dios verdadero.

VIII

Cabeza meditadora,
¡qué lejos se oye el zumbido
de la abeja libadora!

Echaste un velo de sombra
sobre el bello mundo, y vas
creyendo ver, porque mides
la sombra con un compás.

Mientras la abeja fabrica,
melifica,
con jugo de campo y sol,
yo voy echando verdades
que nada son, vanidades
al fondo de mi crisol.
De la mar al percepto,
del percepto al concepto,
del concepto a la idea
—¡oh, la linda tarea!—,
de la idea a la mar.
¡Y otra vez a empezar!

The God whom we all bear,
conceived by all mankind,
the God that we all seek
and whom we shall never find.
Three the gods or three the persons
in the one true God combined.

Head, thinking endlessly,
how faroff is the droning
of the sipping honeybee!

You throw a veil of shadow
on the lovely world; presumptuous,
believe you see because you measure
shadow with a compass.

Working in the fields all sunny,
making honey
from field and sun reducible,
while I go tossing verities
that are nothing, only vanities,
into the pit of my crucible.
From the ocean to the perception,
from the perception to the conception,
from the concept to the idea—
oh, the beautiful chore!—
from the idea to the sea.
And then to begin once more!

A. McV.

CXXXIX
(A DON FRANCISCO GINER DE LOS RÍOS)

Como se fué el maestro,
la luz de esta mañana
me dijo: Van tres días
que mi hermano Francisco no trabaja.
¿Murió? . . . Sólo sabemos
que se nos fué por una senda clara,
diciéndonos: Hacedme
un duelo de labores y esperanzas.
Sed buenos y no más, sed lo que he sido
entre vosotros: alma.
Vivid, la vida sigue,
los muertos mueren y las sombras pasan;
lleva quien deja y vive el que ha vivido.
¡Yunques, sonad; enmudeced, campanas!

Y hacia otra luz más pura
partió el hermano de la luz del alba,
del sol de los talleres,
el viejo alegre de la vida santa.
. . . Oh, sí, llevad, amigos,
su cuerpo a la montaña,
a los azules montes
del ancho Guadarrama.
Allí hay barrancos hondos
de pinos verdes donde el viento canta.
Su corazón repose
bajo una encina casta,
en tierra de tomillos, donde juegan
mariposas doradas . . .
Allí el maestro un día
soñaba un nuevo florecer de España.

Baeza, 21 febrero, 1915.

CXXXIX

TO DON FRANCISCO GINER DE LOS RÍOS

Now that the master has gone,
the light of morning's rays
said, "My brother Francisco
worked not these past three days.
Has he then died?" . . . We know but this:
he left us, taking a shining road
and saying: "Make for me
a mourning of work and hope.
Be good and no more; be what I have been
among you all: the soul.
Live, for life goes on,
the dead die and shadows dispel;
when the living keep faith, the dead live on.
Anvils, sound! Tolling bells, be still!"

Toward another, more pure dawn
our brother turned from the breaking light,
from the sun-filled studios,
joyous and aged, from a holy life.
Oh, yes, friends, carry his body
high up the mountain side,
up to the blue of the mountains
in the wide Guadarramas' heights.
There are the deep ravines
of verdant pines where the wind sings free.
May his heart find rest below
a chaste encina tree
in a land of thyme where butterflies
frolic on gilt-powdered wings . . .
There the master one day
dreamed his dream of Spain's new flowering.

Baeza, February 21, 1915
A. McV.

171

CXLIV
(UNA ESPAÑA JOVEN)

. . . Fué un tiempo de mentira, de infamia. A España toda,
la malherida España, de Carnaval vestida
nos la pusieron, pobre y escuálida y beoda,
para que no acertara la mano con la herida.

Fué ayer; éramos casi adolescentes; era
con tiempo malo, encinta de lúgubres presagios,
cuando montar quisimos en pelo una quimera,
mientras la mar dormía ahita de naufragios.

Dejamos en el puerto la sórdida galera,
y en una nave de oro nos plugo navegar
hacia los altos mares, sin aguardar ribera,
lanzando velas y anclas y gobernalle al mar.

Ya entonces, por el fondo de nuestro sueño—herencia
de un siglo que vencido sin gloria se alejaba—
un alba entrar quería; con nuestra turbulencia
la luz de las divinas ideas batallaba.

Mas cada cual el rumbo siguió de su locura;
agilitó su brazo, acreditó su brío;
dejó como un espejo bruñida su armadura
y dijo: "El hoy es malo, pero el mañana . . es mío".

Y es hoy aquel mañana de ayer . . . Y España toda,
con sucios oropeles de Carnaval vestida
aun la tenemos: pobre y escuálida y beoda;
mas hoy de un vino malo: la sangre de su herida.

Tú, juventud más joven, si de más alta cumbre
la voluntad te llega, irás a tu aventura
despierta y transparente a la divina lumbre,
como el diamante clara, como el diamante pura.

1914.

A YOUNG SPAIN

A time it was of lies, of infamy. And they
took all suffering Spain, our sorely wounded Spain,
and clothed her in carnival costume, squalid, drunken, poor,
to hide the wounded hand, athrob with pain.

Yesterday it was; we were barely adolescent;
an evil time, girt in lugubrious prophecies,
when we longed to ride bareback upon a chimera, while
the ocean slept from surfeit of shipwrecks on the seas.

We left the sordid galley behind us in the port
and on a golden vessel set forth recklessly
toward high running waves, unheedful of the shores,
with rudder, sails, and anchors, putting forth to sea.

In the background of our dream—a century's heritance,
an age ingloriously doomed, now going forevermore—
a new dawn strove to enter; the light of divine ideas
with our young and headstrong turbulence was waging war.

But each one took the course where his own madness led;
he limbered up his arm, he gloried in his prime;
like a polished mirror each left his armor, saying,
"Though today be evil, tomorrow ... shall be mine."

Today is that morrow of yesterday ... And still we have
all Spain in the bedraggled tinsel of carnival dress,
poor and squalid and drunken—oh, but worse—today
on the poorest of wine: her wound in all its bloodiness.

If you, still younger youth, are taken by your will
venturing from a higher peak, you will go right,
to divine light receptive, transparent and awake,
like the diamond, pure, like the diamond, bright.

1914
A. McV.

CXLVIII
(A LA MUERTE DE RUBÉN DARÍO)

Si era toda en tu verso la armonía del mundo,
¿dónde fuiste, Darío, la armonía a buscar?
Jardinero de Hesperia, ruiseñor de los mares,
corazón asombrado de la música astral,
¿te ha llevado Dionysos de su mano al infierno
y con las nuevas rosas triunfante volverás?
¿Te han herido buscando la soñada Florida,
la fuente de la eterna juventud, capitán?
Que en esta lengua madre la clara historia quede;
corazones de todas las Españas, llorad.
Rubén Darío ha muerto en sus tierras de Oro,
esta nueva nos vino atravesando el mar.
Pongamos, españoles, en un severo mármol,
su nombre, flauta y lira, y una inscripción no más:
nadie esta lira pulse, si no es el mismo Apolo,
nadie esta flaute suene, si no es el mismo Pan.

(1916).

CL
(MIS POETAS)

El primero es Gonzalo de Berceo llamado,
Gonzalo de Berceo, poeta y peregrino,
que yendo en romería acaeció en un prado,
y a quien los sabios pintan copiando un pergamino.

Trovó a Santo Domingo, trovó a Santa María,
y a San Millán, y a San Lorenzo y Santa Oria,
y dijo: mi dictado non es de juglaría;
escrito lo tenemos; es verdadera historia.

Su verso es dulce y grave: monótonas hileras,
de chopos invernales en donde nada brilla;
renglones como surcos en pardas sementeras,
y lejos, las montañas azules de Castilla.

174

CXLVIII
ON THE DEATH OF RUBÉN DARÍO

If all the world's harmony was in your verse, Darío,
where then have you gone in search of harmony?
Hesperian gardener, ocean's nightingale,
your heart wonder-struck by astral melodies,
has Dionysius with his hand taken you to hell
and will you, with new roses, return triumphantly?
Captain, were you wounded seeking the fount of youth,
that fount in Florida of dreamed mythology?
To keep the radiant tale within the mother-tongue,
O hearts of all the Spains, weep now for this man.
The sorrowful news has traveled across the sea to us:
Rubén Darío died there in his golden land.
O Spaniards, let us carve on an austere marble block
his name, a flute and lyre, and no words other than:
None may stroke this lyre, save he be Apollo,
none may sound this flute if he be not Pan.

(1916)
A. McV.

CL
MY POETS

The first one is called Gonzalo de Berceo,
Gonzalo de Berceo, poet and peregrine,
who, on a pilgrimage, chanced upon a meadow
and, copying parchments, in portraits can be seen.

He sang to Santo Domingo, he sang to Santa María,
to San Millán, San Lorenzo, and to Santa Oria,
and said: "What I am writing is not mere minstrelsy;
we have it writ full well: truthful history."

His verse is dulcet, grave; monotony of rows
of winter poplars lacking brilliancy's appeal;
his lines are like furrows opened in a field
and, in the distance, blue mountains of Castile.

175

El nos cuenta el repaire del romeo cansado;
leyendo en santorales y libros de oración,
copiando historias viejas, nos dice su dictado,
mientras le sale afuera la luz del corazón.

CLII
(A JUAN RAMÓN JIMÉNEZ)
Por su libro *Arias tristes.*

Era una noche del mes
de mayo, azul y serena.
Sobre el agudo ciprés
brillaba la luna llena,

iluminando la fuente
en donde el agua surtía
sollozando intermitente.
Sólo la fuente se oía.

Después, se escuchó el acento
de un oculto ruiseñor.
Quebró una racha de viento
la curva del surtidor.

Y una dulce melodía
vagó por todo el jardín:
entre los mirtos tañía
un músico su violín.

Era un acorde lamento
de juventud y de amor
para la luna y el viento,
el agua y el ruiseñor.

"El jardín tiene una fuente
y la fuente una quimera . . ."
Cantaba una voz doliente,
alma de la primavera.

He tells us the relaxation the weary pilgrim takes:
reading lives of saints, reading prayer books; then,
copying history, records his inspiration
while a light within his heart shines outwardly toward men.

A. McV.

CLII
TO JUAN RAMÓN JIMÉNEZ

For his book *Arias tristes*

A night in the month of May,
serene and blue of tone.
Over the sharp-edged cypress
the brilliant full moon shone,

illuminating the fount
where the water surged,
weeping intermittently.
Only the fountain was heard,

till the voice of a nightingale
sounded through moonlit dark.
A gust of wind broke off
the water's flowing arc.

And a dulcet melody
wandered flowering land:
a violin among myrtles,
played by an expert hand.

A lament it played, of youth
and love, melodious tale
meant for moon and wind,
water and nightingale.

"The garden has a fountain
and the fountain a chimera ..."
A grieving voice sang,
the heart of primavera.

177

Calló la voz y el violín
apagó su melodía.
Quedó la melancolía
vagando por el jardín.
Sólo la fuente se oía.

CLIII

(OLIVO DEL CAMINO)

A la memoria de D. Cristóbal Torres.

VII

La madre de la bella Proserpina
trocó en moreno grano,
para el sabroso pan de blanca harina,
aguas de abril y soles del verano.

Trigales y trigales ha corrido
la rubia diosa de la hoz dorada,
y del campo a las eras del ejido,
con sus montes de mies agavillada,
llegaron los huesudos bueyes rojos,
la testa dolorida al yugo atada,
y con la tarde ubérrima en los ojos.

De segados trigales y alcaceles
hizo el fuego sequizos rastrojales;
en el huerto rezuma el higo mieles,
cuelga la oronda pera en los perales,
hay en las vides rubios moscateles,
y racimos de rosa en los parrales
que festonan la blanca almacería
de los huertos. Ya irá de glauca a bruna,
por llano, loma, alcor y serranía,
de los verdes olivos la aceituna . . .

Stilled was the violin,
quenched were the singing words.
But melancholy stirred,
roaming through the garden.
Only the fountain was heard.

A. McV.

CLIII

OLIVE TREE BY THE ROAD

To the memory of D. Cristóbal Torres

VII

The mother of lovely Persephone
bargained with tawny grain
for bread of white flour, delectable,
the suns of summer and April rain.

Through field after wheatfield has she run,
the goddess fair with her sickle of gold;
big-boned and red, the oxen have come
from field to threshing floor; untold
the mountains of sheaves, and firmly lies
on doleful head the well placed yoke,
and they hold the bountiful day in their eyes.

To fields of stubble the fire strips
the gleaned, the arid wheat and barley fields;
from garden figs the honey drips,
and rounded pears the pear tree yields.
Light muscatel grapes hang on the vine;
there are rose-colored stems in filigree,
over small garden oil press they entwine.
And now has the oil of the olives begun
to cross the plain, hill and peak to climb,
and the colors are gray to frosty plum.

179

Tu fruto, ¡oh polvoriento del camino
árbol ahito de la estiva llama!,
no estrujarán las piedras del molino,
aguardará la fiesta, en la alta rama,
del alegre zorzal, o el estornino
lo llevará en su pico, alborozado.

Que en tu ramaje luzca, árbol sagrado,
bajo la luna llena,
el ojo encandilado
del buho insomne de la sabia Atena.

Y que la diosa de la hoz bruñida
y de la adusta frente
materna sed y angustia de uranida
traiga a tu sombra, olivo de la fuente.

Y con tus ramas la divina hoguera
encienda en un hogar del campo mío,
por donde tuerce perezoso un río
que toda la campiña hace ribera
antes que un pueblo, hacia la mar, navío.

CLIV
(APUNTES)

IX

Los olivos grises,
los caminos blancos.
El sol ha sorbido
la color del campo;
y hasta tu recuerdo
me lo va secando
este alma de polvo
de los días malos.

Your fruit, O tree here in the dust
of the road, replete with summer's flame,
the stones of the mill, they shall not crush;
it shall wait the fiesta, high in the tree,
of the merry thrush, or the starling may
bear it off in her beak, rejoicingly.

May your leaves be lit, O sacred tree,
with the full moon in the sky,
by the owl of wise Athene
with his dazzling, never-sleeping eye.

And may she, goddess of burnished sickle
and of the brow austere,
bring maternal thirst and celestial pain
to the shade you cast by the little spring here.

A fire divine may your branches be,
to burn on a hearth in that land of mine
through which a river will lazily wind,
making fields a shore beside the sea
and seaside town to ship be redesigned.

A. McV.

C L I V
NOTES

IX

Gray olive trees,
white the roads run,
countryside colors
drained by the sun;
even thy memory
under these rays
shrivels to dust
of evil days.

A. McV.

CLV
(HACIA TIERRA BAJA)

I

Rejas de hierro; rosas de grana.
¿A quién esperas,
con esos ojos y esas ojeras,
enjauladita como las fieras,
tras de los hierros de tu ventana?

Entre las rejas y los rosales,
¿sueñas amores
de bandoleros galanteadores,
fieros amores entre puñales?

Rondar tu calle nunca verás
ese que esperas; porque se fué
toda la España de Merimée.

Por esta calle—tú elegirás—
pasa un notario
que va al tresillo del boticario,
y un usurero, a su rosario.

También yo paso, viejo y tristón.
Dentro del pecho llevo un león.

II

Aunque me ves por la calle,
también yo tengo mis rejas,
mis rejas y mis rosales.

CLVI
(GALERÍAS)

I

En el azul la banda
de unos pájaros negros
que chillan, aletean y se posan
en el álamo yerto.

CLV
TOWARD THE LOWLAND

I

Rejas of iron; roses of scarlet.
For whom, my child,
with those eyes, those dark-shadowed eyes,
caged like the beasts of the wild,
do you watch from behind iron bars?

In the midst of roses and *rejas*,
of what are you brooding,
of bandits come wooing, pursuing,
fierce loves amid flashing daggers?

You never shall see pass your grille
the one whom you wait: it has gone, gone away,
all of the Spain of Mérimée.

Through this street—choose as you will—
goes the notary there,
to the druggist's for card games he shares,
and the usurer, bound for his prayers.

I, too, pass by, old and depressed,
bearing a lion within my breast.

II

Though you see me out here on the street,
I, too, have my iron bars,
my *rejas* and my roses sweet.

A. McV.

CLVI
GALLERIES

I

In the blue a flock
of black birds noisily
screaming, flapping, settle
in rigid poplar tree.

... En el desnudo álamo,
las graves chovas quietas y en silencio,
cual negras, frías notas
escritas en la pauta de febrero.

II

El monte azul, el río, las erectas
varas cobrizas de los finos álamos,
y el blanco del almendro en la colina,
¡oh nieve en flor y mariposa en árbol!
Con el aroma del habar, el viento
corre en la alegre soledad del campo.

III

Una centella blanca
en la nube de plomo culebrea.
¡Los asombrados ojos
del niño, y juntas cejas
—está el salón obscuro—de la madre!...
¡Oh cerrado balcón a la tormenta!
El viento aborrascado y el granizo
en el limpio cristal repiquetean.

IV

El iris y el balcón.
                    Las siete cuerdas
de la lira del sol vibran en sueños.
Un tímpano infantil da siete golpes
—agua y cristal—.
                    Acacias con jilgueros.
Cigüeñas en las torres.
                    En la plaza,
lavó la lluvia el mirto polvoriento.
En el amplio rectángulo ¿quién puso
ese grupo de vírgenes risueño,
y arriba ¡hosanna! entre la rota nube,
la palma de oro y el azul sereno?

In the stark-limbed poplar,
jackdaws grave and, in their silence, very
like to cold black notes
writ on the staff of February.

II

The mountain blue, the river, the straight
coppery twigs of slender poplars
and the white of the hillside almond tree,
oh, butterfly in tree, snow in blossom!
Fragrant with beanfields, the running wind
in the blithe solitude of the open frolics.

III

Lightning streaking white
serpentines through the leaden cloud.
Startled eyes of the child
and the worried line of the brows—
for dark is the room—of the mother.
Oh, balcony closed till the storm should pass!
The storm-blown wind and beating hail
pounding upon the sparkling glass.

IV

Iris and balcony.
    The seven chords
of the sun's bright lyre are playing dreamily.
A childish drum is giving seven rolls—
water and glass.
    Linnets in acacia trees.
Storks upon the towers.
    In the plaza
the dusty myrtle tree wears rain-washed hues.
Who placed in the wide rectangle of the plaza
those smiling virgins gathered in a group
and above—hosannah!—there in the torn cloud
the golden palm and the tranquil blue?

185

Entre montes de almagre y peñas grises,
el tren devora su rail de acero.
La hilera de brillantes ventanillas
lleva un doble perfil de camafeo,
tras el cristal de plata, repetido ...
¿Quién ha punzado el corazón del tiempo?

¿Quién puso, entre las rocas de ceniza,
para la miel del sueño,
esas retamas de oro
y esas azules flores del romero?
La sierra de violeta
y, en el poniente, el azafrán del cielo,
¿quién ha pintado? ¡El abejar, la ermita,
el tajo sobre el río, el sempiterno
rodar del agua entre las hondas peñas,
y el rubio verde de los campos nuevos,
y todo, hasta la tierra blanca y rosa
al pie de los almendros!

En el silencio sigue
la lira pitagórica vibrando,
el iris en la luz, la luz que llena
mi estereoscopio vano.
Han cegado mis ojos las cenizas
del fuego heraclitano.
El mundo es, un momento,
transparente, vacío, ciego, alado.

CLVII
(LA LUNA, LA SOMBRA Y EL BUFÓN)

I

Fuera, la luna platea
cúpulas, torres, tejados;

Passing through mountains of ochre and ashen rocks,
the train devours its steely line.
The file of glittering windows bears
cameos doubled in profiled design,
beyond the silver panes repeated . . .
Who has pierced the very heart of time?

VI

Who was it that placed among the ash-gray rocks
for honey of dreaming hours
that furze of golden yellow,
those rosemary shrubs revealing their azure flowers?
The sierra of violet
and, in the setting sun, the saffron of the sky,
who painted them? Beehive and hermitage,
cliff rising over the river, the lazuli
of water eternally rolling among deep rocks,
the golden green of newly growing fields,
and all the scene, even the pink and white earth
at the foot of the almond trees!

VII

In the silence the Pythagorean
lyre throbs, remote,
rainbow in light, the light that fills
my useless stereoscope.
Ashes from Hercules' fire
my eyes have blinded, singed.
The world is, for a moment,
transparent, empty, blind, and winged.

A. McV.

CLVII
MOON, SHADOW, AND BUFFOON

I

Cupolas, towers, rooftops,
outside the moon is changing

dentro, mi sombra pasea
por los muros encalados.
Con esta luna, parece
que hasta la sombra envejece.

Ahorremos la serenata
de una cenestesia ingrata,
y una vejez intranquila,
y una luna de hojalata.
Cierra tu balcón, Lucila.

II

Se pintan panza y joroba
en la pared de mi alcoba.
Canta el bufón:
        ¡Qué bien van,
en un rostro de cartón,
unas barbas de azafrán!
Lucila, cierra el balcón.

CLVIII
(CANCIONES DE TIERRAS ALTAS)

I

Por la sierra blanca . . .
La nieve menuda
y el viento de cara.

Por entre los pinos . . .
con la blanca nieve
se borra el camino.

Recio viento sopla
de Urbión a Moncayo.
¡Páramos de Soria!

II

Ya habrá cigüeñas al sol,
mirando la tarde roja,
entre Moncayo y Urbión.

188

to silver and, within,
on walls my shadow pacing.
With this moon, it seems
the very shadow is aging.

From unwelcome coenesthesia
let us save the serenade,
from old age all uneasy
and a moon of tin plate made.
Close your window, Lucille.

II

Paunch and humpback painted
on bedroom wall of white.
Sings the buffoon:
                    Becoming
to your cartoon face indeed
is the saffron beard tonight.
Close the window, Lucille.

                              A. McV.

CLVIII

SONGS OF THE HIGHLANDS

I

White peaks in a row . . .
Wind in one's face
and fine-sifted snow.

Pines thickly placed . . .
by the white snow,
the pathway erased.

Harsh winds will have pressed
from Moncayo to Urbión.
The Sorian steppes!

II

Now there'll be storks in the sun
from Moncayo to Urbión,
watching the red twilight come.

189

Se abrió la puerta que tiene
gonces en mi corazón,
y otra vez la galería
de mi historia apareció.

Otra vez la plazoleta
de las acacias en flor,
y otra vez la fuente clara
cuenta un romance de amor.

X

(IRIS DE LA NOCHE)

A D. Ramón del Valle-Inclán.

Hacia Madrid, una noche,
va el tren por el Guadarrama.
En el cielo, el arco iris
que hacen la luna y el agua.
¡Oh luna de abril, serena,
que empuja las nubes blancas!

La madre lleva a su niño,
dormido, sobre la falda.
Duerme el niño y, todavía,
ve el campo verde que pasa,
y arbolillos soleados,
y mariposas doradas.

La madre, ceño sombrío
entre un ayer y un mañana,
ve unas ascuas mortecinas
y una hornilla con arañas.

Hay un trágico viajero,
que debe ver cosas raras,
y habla solo y, cuando mira,
nos borra con la mirada.

Yo pienso en campos de nieve
y en pinos de otras montañas.

Once more that door reveals
the gallery hid inside—
its hinges in my heart,
that door has opened wide.

Once more the tiny plaza,
the acacia flowers thereof,
once more the fountain bright
telling a tale of love.

A. McV.

X

NIGHT RAINBOW

To D. Ramón del Valle-Inclán

Through the Guadarramas by night,
to Madrid the train is passing.
Arched in the sky, a rainbow
by moon and water fashioned.
Oh, April moon, serenely
pushing the white cloud masses.

A child in his mother's lap
gently sleeping lies
yet through his slumber sees
green countryside pass by,
and little sun-tinged trees,
and gilded butterflies.

'Twixt a yesterday and a morrow
the mother, with troubled brow
sees spider webs on a hearth
and embers dying out.

Here is a tragic traveler;
strange things his thoughts devise.
He talks alone, and looking,
erases us with his eyes.

I think of snowy fields,
of other slopes with pines.

Y tú, Señor, por quien todos
vemos y que ves las almas,
dinos si todos, un día,
hemos de verte la cara.

CLIX
(CANCIONES)

I

Junto a la sierra florida,
bulle el ancho mar.
El panal de mis abejas
tiene granitos de sal.

II

Junto al agua negra.
Olor de mar y jazmines.
Noche malagueña.

III

La primavera ha venido.
Nadie sabe cómo ha sido.

IV

La primavera ha venido.
¡Aleluyas blancas
de los zarzales floridos!

V

¡Luna llena, luna llena,
tan oronda, tan redonda
en esta noche serena
de marzo, panal de luz
que labran blancas abejas!

And Thou, Lord, through whom we see,
who our hearts canst trace,
tell us if one day we
shall look upon Thy face.

A. McV.

CLIX
SONGS

I

By the sierra gardens
the wide seas break in foam,
and grains of salt I find
within the honeycomb.

II

By waters flowing darkly.
Night over Málaga.
Sea foam and jasmine blowing.

III

Suddenly—spring is here!
No one saw her appear.

IV

Now comes the spring.
Blossoms of briers upon the air
white hosannas fling!

V

Full moon, full moon,
glory-crowned, so very round,
in this peaceful, springtime night,
white bees are building you
a honeycomb of light!

Noche castellana;
la canción se dice,
o, mejor, se calla.
Cuando duerman todos,
saldré a la ventana.

Canta, canta en claro rimo,
el almendro en verde rama
y el doble sauce del rió.

Canta de la parda encina
la rama que el hacha corta,
y la flor que nadie mira.

De los perales del huerto
la blanca flor, la rosada
flor de melocotonero.

Y este olor
que arranca el viento mojado
a los habares en flor.

VIII

La fuente y las cuatro
acacias en flor
de la plazoleta.
Ya no quema el sol.
¡Tardecita alegre!
Canta, ruiseñor.
Es la misma hora
de mi corazón.

¡Blanca hospedería,
celda de viajero,
con la sombra mía!

VI

Castilian evening . . .
The music will begin,
or better, cease to sing.
To the window will I come
when all are slumbering.

VII

Singing and keeping time,
river willow and green
almond bough sing a rhyme.

They sing of gray oak tree
with branch for axe to fell,
and flowers none may see.

White flowers of the pear,
pink flowers of the peach,
in gardens everywhere.

And of this perfume
by winged, wet winds carried
from bean fields in bloom.

VIII

Above the little square
the sun no longer burns.
With the four acacias
to dusk the fountain turns.
O happy afternoon!
Sing, nightingale, thy rue!
In my heart this hour
it is twilight too.

IX

On whitewashed walls
of the traveler's cell,
my shadow falls.

XIII

Hay fiesta en el prado verde
—pífano y tambor .
Con su cayado florido
y abarcas de oro vino un pastor.

Del monte bajé,
sólo por bailar con ella;
al monte me tornaré.

En los árboles del huerto
hay un ruiseñor;
canta de noche y de día,
canta a la luna y al sol.
Ronco de cantar;
el huerto vendrá la niña
y una rosa cortará.

Entre las negras encinas,
hay una fuente de piedra,
y un cantarillo de barro
que nunca se llena.

Por el encinar,
con la blanca luna,
ella volverá.

XV

Mientras danzáis en corro,
niñas, cantad:
Ya están los prados verdes,
ya vino abril galán.

A la orilla del río,
por el negro encinar,
sus abarcas de plata
hemos visto brillar.
Ya están los prados verdes,
ya vino abril galán.

In meadows green they dance
to sound of fifes and drums.
With sandals gold and crook
in bud, a shepherd comes.

From hills in haste came I,
only to dance with her;
back to the hills I'll hie.

Among the garden trees
there is a nightingale.
By night and day, to sun
and moon he tells his tale.
The bird in garden close
is hoarse with song. The maid
will come to pluck a rose.

Among the oak trees black
there is a fountain stilled,
a little jar of clay
that never has been filled.

With the white moon
through groves of oak,
she will come soon.

XV

While you dance in a ring,
maidens, sing.
Now green the meadows are,
now comes the wooing spring.

Among the oak trees black,
by river murmuring,
where tread his sandaled feet,
the silver traces cling.
Now green the meadows are,
now comes the wooing spring.

F. L. M.

CLX
(CANCIONES DEL ALTO DUERO)

Canción de mozas.

I

Molinero es mi amante,
tiene un molino
bajo los pinos verdes,
cerca del río.
Niñas, cantad:
"Por la orilla del Duero
yo quisiera pasar."

II

Por las tierras de Soria
va mi pastor.
¡Si yo fuera una encina
sobre un alcor!
Para la siesta,
si yo fuera una encina
sombra le diera.

III

Colmenero es mi amante
y en su abejar,
abejicas de oro
vienen y van.
De tu colmena,
colmenero del alma,
yo colmenera.

IV

En las sierras de Soria,
azul y nieve,
leñador es mi amante
de pinos verdes.
¡Quién fuera el águila
para ver a mi dueño
cortando ramas!

198

CLX

SONGS OF THE UPPER DUERO

Song of the girls

I

A miller is my love
and he has a mill
under green of pine trees
where the waters spill.
Girls, sing with me:
"By the River Duero
I should like to be."

II

There's my shepherd walking
over Soria land.
Oh, to be an oak tree
and on a hill to stand!
At siesta I should be
the one to give him shade,
if I were a tree.

III

A beekeeper is my love
and his full hives hold,
between their busy journeys,
little bees of gold.
Of your apiary,
beekeeper of the heart,
guardian I would be.

IV

In the Sorian mountains,
blue and snowy scene,
my lover is a woodsman,
cutting pine trees green.
Oh, to soar above,
to be an eagle, watching
the woodsman of my love!

V

Hortelano es mi amante,
tiene su huerto,
en la tierra de Soria,
cerca del Duero.
¡Linda hortelana!
Llevaré saya verde,
monjil de grana.

VI

A la orilla del Duero,
lindas peonzas,
bailad, coloraditas
como amapolas.

¡Ay, garabí!...
Bailad, suena la flauta
y el tamboril.

C L X I
(PROVERBIOS Y CANTARES)

A José Ortega y Gasset.

XL

Los ojos por que suspiras,
sábelo bien,
los ojos en que te miras
son ojos porque te ven.

XLIX

¿Dijiste media verdad?
Dirán que mientes dos veces
si dices la otra mitad.

200

A gardener is my love;
here in Soria land
he cherishes his garden
near the Duero's strand.
Pretty garden maid!
I'll wear a scarlet robe
and a skirt of jade.

Pretty spinning tops,
dance on Duero's shore,
as crimson is your color
as ever poppies wore.

Ay, tum-ti-tum!
Dance; the flute is calling,
and the little drum.

A. McV.

CLXI

PROVERBS AND SONGS

To José Ortega y Gasset

XL

The eyes for which you are sighing,
it is true,
the eyes in which you see yourself
are eyes, for they see you.

XLIX

Was it half a truth you told?
If you tell the other half
they'll say your lie's twofold.

LV

Ya hubo quien pensó:
cogito ergo non sum.
¡Qué exageración!

LVIII

Creí mi hogar apagado,
y revolví la ceniza . . .
Me quemé la mano.

LXVI

Poned atención:
un corazón solitario
no es un corazón.

LXVIII

Todo necio
confunde valor y precio.

LXXXV

¿Tu verdad? No, la Verdad,
y ven conmigo a buscarla.
La tuya, guárdatela.

LXXXVIII

El pensamiento barroco
pinta virutas de fuego,
hincha y complica el decoro.

LXXXIX

Sin embargo . . .
                    —Oh, sin embargo,
hay siempre un ascua de veras
en su incendio de teatro.

XCIV

Doy consejo, a fuer de viejo:
nunca sigas mi consejo.

LV

There was one who tried meditation:
cogito ergo non sum.
Now there's an exaggeration!

LVIII

The ash on my hearth I turned,
believing the fire was out . . .
My hand was burned.

LXVI

Your attention I call:
a solitary heart
is no heart at all.

LXVIII

All vice
confounds value and price.

LXXXV

Your truth? No, the Truth,
come now with me to seek it.
As for your own, keep it.

LXXXVIII

The baroque mind will immure
spirals of flame in paint,
inflate and twist the pure.

LXXXIX

Nevertheless . . .
        —Oh, nevertheless,
in the burning of a theater
an ash of truth is left.

XCIV

With advice I proceed, being old indeed:
advice I advise you never to heed.

203

Pero tampoco es razón
desdeñar
consejo que es confesión.

CLXIV
(GLOSANDO A RONSARD Y OTRAS RIMAS)

AL ESCULTOR EMILIANO BARRAL

... Y tu cincel me esculpía
en una piedra rosada,
que lleva una aurora fría
eternamente encantada.
Y la agria melancolía
de una soñada grandeza,
que es lo español (fantasía
con que adobar la pereza),
fué surgiendo de esa roca,
que es mi espejo,
línea a línea, plano a plano,
y mi boca de sed poca,
y, so el arco de mi cejo,
dos ojos de un ver lejano,
que yo quisiera tener
como están en tu escultura:
cavados en piedra dura,
en piedra, para no ver.

(p.334-335)

LOS SUEÑOS DIALOGADOS

I

¡Como en el alto llano tu figura
se me aparece! ... Mi palabra evoca
el prado verde y la árida llanura,
la zarza en flor, la cenicienta roca.

But neither should you transgress
by showing disdain
when, by advising, I confess.

A. McV.

CLXIV

VARIATIONS ON RONSARD AND OTHER RHYMES

TO THE SCULPTOR EMILIANO BARRAL

And out of rose-tinted stone
your chisel fashioned me,
of stone with the chill of dawn,
enchanted eternally.
The bitter melancholy
of dreamed-of greatness is there,
so Spanish (fantasy hiding
the true lethargic air),
it surged from that rock, that mirror,
revealing my face as such,
line by line and plane by plane,
my mouth that thirsts not much
and under arched brows two eyes
with a farseeing quality.
Would that, as in the sculpture,
these eyes could be for me
carved from solid rock,
of stone, so as not to see.

A. McV.

DREAM CONVERSATIONS

I

As once upon the high plateau, again
I see your face! ... The scene that we have known
comes as I speak: green pastures, arid plain,
the flowering thorn, the heaps of ash-gray stone.

Y al recuerdo obediente, negra encina
brota en el cerro, baja el chopo al río;
el pastor va subiendo a la colina;
brilla un balcón de la ciudad: el mío,

el nuestro. ¿Ves? Hacia Aragón, lejana,
la sierra de Moncayo, blanca y rosa . . .
Mira el incendio de esa nube grana,

y aquella estrella en el azul, esposa.
Tras el Duero, la loma de Santana
se amorata en la tarde silenciosa.

(p.342-343)

CLXV
(SONETOS)

II

Verás la maravilla del camino,
camino de soñada Compostela
—¡oh monte lila y flavo!—, peregrino,
en un llano, entre chopos de candela.

Otoño con dos ríos ha dorado
el cerco del gigante centinela
de piedra y luz, prodigio torreado
que en el azul sin mancha se modela.

Verás en la llanura una jauría
de agudos galgos y un señor de caza,
cabalgando a lejana serranía,

vano fantasma de una vieja raza.
Debes entrar cuando en la tarde fría
brille un balcón de la desierta plaza.

Beside the river, docile memory shows
a poplar; an oak tree breaks the hillside line
with black; uphill the weary shepherd goes;
a balcony shines from the city: mine,

and ours. You see? Toward Aragón, afar,
the mountains of Moncayo, rose and white.
Look up, my wife, through blue sky comes a star

and in the west the sunset clouds ignite.
Santana hill, beyond the Duero's bar,
grows purple in the afternoon's still light.

J. R. L.

CLXV
SONNETS

II

Behold the roadway's miracle fulfilled,
the road where dreamed-of Compostela lies,
pilgrim,—a mountain, lilac and untilled—
between the poplars which like candles rise.

With rivers twain has autumn gilded bright
a halo for this tower of giant size,
prodigious sentinel of stone and light,
massive against the cloudless, azure skies.

See on the plain each lean and hungry hound,
the pack, where rides the master of the chase
unto a distant range of mountains bound,

vain phantom of a proud and ancient race;
you should go in when night grows cold around
a window shining in that lonely place.

E. D. T.

CLXVI
(VIEJAS CANCIONES)

I

A la hora del rocío,
de la niebla salen
sierra blanca y prado verde.
¡El sol en los encinares!

Hasta borrarse en el cielo,
suben las alondras.
¿Quién puso plumas al campo?
¿Quién hizo alas de tierra loca?

Al viento, sobre la sierra,
tiene el águila dorada
las anchas alas abiertas.

Sobre la picota
donde nace el río,
sobre el lago de turquesa
y los barrancos de verdes pinos;
sobre veinte aldeas,
sobre cien caminos . . .

Por los senderos del aire,
señora águila,
¿donde vais a todo vuelo tan de mañana?

II

Ya había un albor de luna
en el cielo azul.
¡La luna en los espartales,
cerca de Alicún!
Redonda sobre el alcor,
y rota en las turbias aguas
del Guadiana menor.

CLXVI
OLD SONGS

I

When the dew is falling,
out of mist they come,
white peaks and grassy pastures.
The oak groves catch the sun.

Until the sky effaces them,
the larks soar high and fast.
Who dropped those feathers on the field?
Who fashioned wings from foolish land?

The golden eagle holds
her wide untiring wings
outspread to mountain winds.

Above the mountain top,
the birthplace of the river,
above the turquoise lake
and green pines in the fissures,
above a score of towns,
above a hundred roads . . .

Along the lanes of air,
Madam Eagle, say,
where do you fly so fast, so early in the day?

II

Upon the deep blue sky
appeared the rising moon.
The moon among the matweeds
close by Alicún.
Rounded on the knolls,
and down the Guadiana,
shattered on the shoals.

Entre Ubeda y Baeza
—loma de las dos hermanas:
Baeza, pobre y señora,
Ubeda, reina y gitana—.
Y en el encinar,
¡luna redonda y beata,
siempre conmigo a la par!

CLXVII

DE UN CANCIONERO APÓCRIFO

CONSEJOS, COPLAS, APUNTES

9

La plaza tiene una torre,
la torre tiene un balcón,
el balcón tiene una dama,
la dama una blanca flor.
Ha pasado un caballero,
—¡quién sabe por qué pasó!—,
y se ha llevado la plaza
con su torre y su balcón,
con su balcón y su dama,
su dama y su blanca flor.

(p.371)

Between Ubeda and Baeza
—two sisters share a hill:
Baeza, impoverished lady,
Queen Ubeda, gypsy still—.
And through the oaks I see
the blessed rounded moon,
keeping pace with me.

J. R. L.

CLXVII
FROM AN APOCRYPHAL ANTHOLOGY
COUNSELS, RHYMES, NOTES

9

A tower belongs to the plaza,
a balcony to the tower,
the balcony has a lady,
and the lady, a white flower.
A gentleman has passed—
who knows why he came by!—
He has taken away the plaza,
the balcony and its tower,
and the lady on the balcony,
the lady and her white flower.

A. McV.

CLXXII
(ABEL MARTÍN)

LOS COMPLEMENTARIOS
(CANCIONERO APÓCRIFO)
RECUERDOS DE SUEÑO, FIEBRE Y DUERMIVELA

I

Esta maldita fiebre
que todo me lo enreda,
siempre diciendo: ¡claro!
Dormido estás: despierta.
¡Masón, masón!
            Las torres
bailando están en rueda.
Los gorriones pían
bajo la lluvia fresca.
¡Oh, claro, claro, claro!
Dormir es cosa vieja,
y el toro de la noche
bufando está a la puerta.
A tu ventana llego
con una rosa nueva,
con una estrella roja
y la garganta seca.
¡Oh, claro, claro, claro!
¿Velones? En Lucena.
¿Cuál de las tres? Son una
Lucía, Inés, Carmela;
y el limonero baila
con la encinilla negra.
¡Oh, claro, claro, claro!
Dormido estás. Alerta.
Mili, mili, en el viento;
glu-glu, glu-glu, en la arena.
Los tímpanos del alba,
¡qué bien repiquetean!
¡Oh, claro, claro, claro!

CLXXII
(ABEL MARTÍN)

COMPLEMENTARY THINGS
(APOCRYPHAL ANTHOLOGY)
MEMORIES OF DREAM, FEVER AND DROWSINESS

I

This cursed fever,
weaving tangles deep,
always saying: Of course!
Awake, you are asleep.
Mason, Mason!
                    The towers
are wheeling in a dance.
Little sparrows chirp
in the rain's exuberance.
Oh, yes, of course, of course!
Sleep is an ancient rite,
and snorting at the door
is the dark bull of night.
With a new rose in my hand
now to your window come I,
I come with a scarlet star
and with a throat that is dry.
Oh, yes, of course, of course!
Oil lamps? In Lucena.
Which of the three? They are one,
Lucía, Inés, Carmela,
and the lemon tree is dancing
with the little black oak tree.
Oh, yes, of course, of course!
You are sleeping. Waken! See—
whisper, whisper on wind,
gurgle on sandy ground.
The kettle drums of dawn,
how gaily they resound.
Oh, yes, of course, of course!

II

En la desnuda tierra . . .

III

Era la tierra desnuda,
y un frío viento, de cara,
con nieve menuda.

Me eché a caminar
por un encinar de sombra:
la sombra de un encinar.

El sol las nubes rompía
con sus trompetas de plata.
La nieve ya no caía.

La vi un momento asomar
en las torres del olvido.
Quise y no pude gritar.

IV

¡Oh, claro, claro, claro!
Ya están los centinelas
alertos. ¡Y esta fiebre
que todo me lo enreda! . . .
Pero a un hidalgo no
se ahorca; se degüella,
señor verdugo. ¿Duermes?
Masón, masón, despierta.
Nudillos infantiles
y voces de muñecas.

———

¡Tan-tan! Quién llama, di?
—¿Se ahorca a un inocente
en esta casa?
                                —Aquí
se ahorca, simplemente.

II

On the denuded ground . . .

III

The earth was a naked place
and a chilly wind was driving
fine snow in my face.

My course I thereon laid
through a shadowy oak grove,
a grove of oakwood shade.

With silver trumpets blowing,
the sun broke through the clouds.
No longer was it snowing.

I saw her—a moment was all,
in the towers of oblivion;
I tried, but could not call.

IV

Oh, yes, of course, of course.
The sentinels vigil keep.
And this besetting fever
weaves such tangles deep!
But a noble is not hanged,
executioner, instead
he need but lose his head.
Asleep? Then wake to my calls.
Knuckles of little children
and the voices of dolls.

―――――

Rat-tat. Who knocks at the door?
"Are they hanging an innocent **man**
here in this house?"
                              "Of course,
here, as simply as that."

215

¡Qué vozarrón! Remacha
el clavo en la madera.
Con esta fiebre . . . ¡Chito!
Ya hay público a la puerta.
La solución más linda
del último problema.
Vayan pasando, pasen;
que nadie quede fuera.

———

—¡Sambenitado, a un lado!
—¿Eso será por mí?
¿Soy yo el sambenitado,
señor verdugo?

—Sí.

———

¡Oh, claro, claro, claro!
Se da trato de cuerda,
que es lo infantil, y el trompo
de música resuena.
Pero la guillotina,
una mañana fresca . . .
Mejor el palo seco,
y su corbata hecha.
¿Guitarras? No se estilan.
Fagotes y cornetas,
y el gallo de la aurora,
si quiere. ¿La reventa
la hacen los curas? ¡Claro!
¡¡¡Sambenitón, despierta!!!

v

Con esta bendita fiebre
la luna empieza a tocar
su pandereta; y danzar
quiere, a la luna, la liebre.
De encinar en encinar
saltan la alondra y el día.

216

What a loud voice! Now
turn the screw once more.
With this fever . . . Hush!
The public is at the door.
The prettiest solution
for the problem has arrived.
Let them come, let them in,
let none be left outside.

———

"One side, damned heretic!"
"Is it I that you address?
Am I the sentenced heretic,
sir hangman, am I?"
                          "Yes."

———

Oh, yes, of course, of course.
And now the cord is wound—
infantilism—the musical
top will then resound.
But the guillotine,
on a morning heady . . .
Better the barren gallows
and the necktie ready.
Guitars? They are not in style.
Bassoons and bugles blow
and, if you should wish it,
at dawn the cock will crow.
Are the curates reselling their take?
Of course. Heretic, wake!!!

v

With this fever blest
the moon begins to play
her tambourine, and away
the hare would dance, possessed.
From oak to oak they flit,
the lark and dawning day.

217

En la mañana serena
hay un latir de jauría,
que por los montes resuena.
Duerme. ¡Alegría! ¡Alegría!

VI

Junto al agua fría,
en la senda clara,
sombra dará algún día
ese arbolillo en que nadie repara.
Un fuste blanco y cuatro verdes hojas
que, por abril, le cuelga primavera,
y arrastra el viento de noviembre, rojas.
Su fruto, sólo un niño lo mordiera.
Su flor, nadie la vió. ¿Cuándo florece?
Ese arbolillo crece
no más que para el ave de una cita,
ques es alma—canto y plumas—de un instante,
un pajarillo azul y petulante
que a la hora de la tarde lo visita.

VII

¡Qué fácil es volar, qué fácil es!
Todo consiste en no dejar que el suelo
se acerque a nuestros pies.
Valiente hazaña, ¡el vuelo!, ¡el vuelo!, ¡el vuelo!

VIII

¡Volar sin alas donde todo es cielo!
Anota este jocundo
pensamiento: Parar, parar el mundo
entre las puntas de los pies,
y luego darle cuerda del revés,
para verlo girar en el vacío,
coloradito y frío,
y callado—no hay música sin viento—.
¡Claro, claro! ¡Poeta y cornetín
son de tan corto aliento! . . .
Sólo el silencio y Dios cantan sin fin.

218

And on this peaceful morning
the hounds begin to bay
among the echoing mountains.
Sleep. Oh, joy! Be gay!

VI

Beside the water cold,
upon the pathway bright,
one day it will give shade,
that small unheeded tree; of white
its tender wood; four and green the leaves
hung by April in the new springtide,
though snatching November winds will find them red.
Its fruit, only a boy would choose to bite.
It flowered unseen. When was it that occurred?
All for the sake of a bird
does that small tree grow tall and bud and bloom—
for the bird is the heart—song and feathers—coming
suddenly, small, blue-winged and petulant,
at trysting hour every afternoon.

VII

How easy to fly, how easy it is!
And it all consists of refusing to alight
or let earth touch our feet.
Valiant exploit—Flight! Flight! Flight!

VIII

To fly without wings where everything is sky!
Note the sportive mirth
of the thought: To stop, stop the very earth
with only the tips of our toes,
then reverse it to see how it goes,
spinning in emptiness still,
a trifle flushed and chill,
and mute—no music is made without wind.
Of course, of course! Out of breath they must be.
poet and cornetist . . .
Only silence and God sing eternally.

219

Pero caer de cabeza,
en esta noche sin luna,
en medio de esta maleza,
junto a la negra laguna . . .

————

—¿Tú eres Caronte, el fúnebre barquero?
Esa barba limosa . . .
                              —¿Y tú, bergante?
—Un fúnebre aspirante
de tu negra barcaza a pasajero,
que al lago irrebogable se aproxima.
—¿Razón?
              —La ignoro. Ahorcóme un peluquero.
—(Todos pierden memoria en este clima).
—¿Delito?
              —No recuerdo.
                                   —¿Ida, no más?
—¿Hay vuelta?
                     —Sí.
                         —Pues ida y vuelta, ¡claro!
—Sí, claro . . . y no tan claro: eso es muy caro.
Aguarda un momentín, y embarcarás.

X

¡Bajar a los infiernos como el Dante!
¡Llevar por compañero
a un poeta con nombre de lucero!
¡Y este fulgor violeta en el diamante!
Dejad toda esperanza . . . Usted, primero.
¡Oh, nunca, nunca, nunca! Usted delante.

————

Palacios de mármol, jardín con cipreses,
naranjos redondos y palmas esbeltas.
Vueltas y revueltas,
eses y más eses.

220

IX

But to fall headlong
on a night without moon,
in the midst of this brake
by the black lagoon . . .

———

"You are Charon, the funereal oarsman in charge?
That slimy beard . . ."
                              "And you, wretched lad?"
"An aspirant sad
who would board your black, your funereal barge
that goes near the impassable lake."
"Your reason?"
                    "I know not. A hairdresser hanged me."
(They all lose their memories in this clime.)
"And your crime?"
                    "I forget."
                                        "One way, no more?"
"You'll return?"
                    "Yes."
                                "Then a round trip, of course."
"Yes, it is clear . . . though not too clear: It is very dear.
One second and you shall come aboard."

X

Like Dante, down to inferno's worst!
With a comrade from afar,
a poet with the name of a star.
And this brilliant diamond, violet-red.
All hope abandon . . . You go first.
Oh, never, never, never! You go ahead.

———

Marble palaces, garden with cypress trees,
round orange trees and the palms' slenderness.
Turnings and then re-turnings,
S after S after S.

221

"Calle del Recuerdo". Ya otra vez pasamos
por ella. "Glorieta de la Blanca Sor".
"Puerta de la Luna". Por aquí ya entramos.
"Calle del Olvido". Pero ¿adónde vamos
por estas malditas andurrias, señor?

  —Pronto te cansas, poeta.
—"Travesía del Amor" . . .
¡y otra vez la "Plazoleta
del Desengaño Mayor"! . . .

XI

  —Es ella . . . Triste y severa.
Di, más bien, indiferente
como figura de cera.

———

  —Es ella . . . Mira y no mira.
—Pon el oído en su pecho
y, luego, dile: respira.

———

  —No alcanzo hasta el mirador.
—Háblale.
   —Si tú quisieras . . . .
—Más alto.
    —Dame esa flor.
¿No me respondes, bien mío?
¡Nada, nada!
Cuajadita con el frío
se quedó en la madrugada.

XII

  ¡Oh, claro, claro, claro!
Amor siempre se hiela.
¡Y en esa "Calle Larga"
con reja, reja y reja,
cien veces, platicando
con cien galanes, ella!

222

The Street of Remembrance. Again it's been found.
The White Sister Circle. We enter here.
The Gate of the Moon. Through it on down
to Oblivion Street. But where are we bound
through these cursed and devious byways, sir?

"Poet, you tire so soon."
Love's Crossroads meet . . .
And once again the small Plaza
of Greatest Deceit!

XI

"It is she . . . Sad, severe of mien.
Say, rather, indifferent,
like a wax figurine."

———

"It is she . . . She looks yet looks away."
"Put your ear to her breast;
then, 'Breathe,' you must say."

———

"I shall not go up to her balcony."
"Speak to her."
                        "If you wish . . ."
"Louder."
                        "Give me that flower.
My love, you do not reply?"
Not a word, not one.
Congealed, there in the cold,
she remained in the dawning sun.

XII

Oh, of course, of course, of course!
Ever frozen love must be.
And here on Long Street, *rejas*
face each vis-à-vis,
a hundred times, conversing
with a hundred gallants—she!

223

¡Oh, claro, claro, claro!
Amor es calle entera,
con celos, celosías,
canciones a las puertas . . .
Yo traigo un do de pecho
guardado en la cartera.
¿Qué te parece?
                              —Guarda.
Hoy cantan las estrellas,
y nada más.
                        ¿Nos vamos?
—Tira por esa calleja.
—Pero ¿otra vez empezamos?
"Plaza Donde Hila la Vieja".
Tiene esa plaza un relente . . .
¿Seguimos?
                    —Aguarda un poco.
Aquí vive un cura loco
por un lindo adolescente.
Y aquí pena arrepentido,
oyendo siempre tronar,
y viendo serpentear
el rayo que lo ha fundido.
"Calle de la Triste Alcuza".
—Un barrio feo. Gentuza.
¡Alto! . . . "Pretil del Valiente".
—Pregunta en el tres.
                                    —¿Manola?
—Aquí. Pero duerme sola:
está de cuerpo presente.
¡Claro, claro! Y siempre clara,
le da la luna en la cara.
—¿Rezamos?
                      —No. Vamonós.
Si la madeja enredamos
con esta fiebre, ¡por Dios!,
ya nunca la devanamos.
. . . Sí, cuatro igual dos y dos.

Oh, yes, of course, of course.
Love is a street and more,
with jealousies and jalousies
and singing at the door.
I bring a tone up from my chest,
kept in a wallet there . . .
How does it strike you?
     "Do take care.
Today the stars are singing
and nothing more."
     "Shall we go?"
"Dart in where this alley begins."
"But must we again start so?
Plaza Where the Old One Spins.
There is dew on that plaza at present . . .
Shall we go on?"
     "No, wait for a bit.
Here lives a curate, bewitched
by a handsome adolescent.
And here repentance holds sway,
forever hearing the thunder
and seeing the serpentine wonder
of the jagged, fusing ray.
"Street of the Grieving Cruet."
"Genteel. Ugliness through it.
Stop! . . . "The Valiant's Rail."
"Ask at the third house."
     "Manola?"
"Here. But she sleeps alone:
her body is lying in grace.
Of course, of course! And always bright,
the moon is shining on her face."
"Shall we pray?"
     "No, let us go.
If we should entangle the skein
with this fever, it would not do.
By Heaven, we'd not free it again.
Yes, four equals two and two."
     A. McV.

225

CLXXIII
(CANCIONES A GUIOMAR)

II

Por ti la mar ensaya olas y espumas,
y el iris, sobre el monte, otros colores,
y el faisán de la aurora canto y plumas,
y el buho de Minerva ojos mayores.
Por ti, ¡oh, Guiomar!...

OBRAS SUELTAS

SONETOS

V

De mar a mar entre los dos la guerra,
más honda que la mar. En mi parterre,
miro a la mar que el horizonte cierra.
Tu asomada, Guiomar, a un finisterre,

miras hacia otro mar, la mar de España
que Camoens cantara, tenebrosa.
Acaso a ti mi ausencia te acompaña,
a mi me duele tu recuerdo, diosa.

La guerra dió al amor el tajo fuerte.
Y es la total angustia de la muerte,
con la sombra infecunda de la llama

y la soñada miel de amor tardío,
y la flor imposible de la rama
que ha sentido del hacha el corte frío.

CLXXIII
SONGS TO GUIOMAR

II

For thee the sea essays waves and spume,
the iris over the peak new colors tries,
the pheasant of the dawn, song and plume,
and the owl of Minerva, greater eyes.
For thee, O Guiomar! . . .

A. McV.

ADDITIONAL WORKS

SONNETS

V

From sea to sea, between us two lies war,
still deeper than the sea. On my parterre
I seaward look, the skyline closed offshore
while thou, Guiomar, thou see'st a finisterre,

facing another sea, that Spanish sea
Camões might have sung in dark-toned line.
Perhaps my absence may accompany thee.
Thy memory, it hurts me, goddess mine.

With mighty strength the war our love has cleft,
and now it is the total pain of death,
the fire's shadow, infecundity,

and love's dreamed honey, overlong delayed,
the impossible flower of the riven tree
that felt the chilling cut of the ax's blade.

A. McV.

EL CRIMEN FUÉ EN GRANADA

Se le vió, caminando entre fusiles,
por una calle larga,
salir al campo frío,
aún con estrellas, de la madrugada.
Mataron a Federico
cuando la luz asomaba.
El pelotón de verdugos
no osó mirarle la cara.
Todos cerraron los ojos;
rezaron: ¡ni Dios te salva!
Muerto cayó Federico
—sangre en la frente y plomo en las entrañas—
... Que fué en Granada el crimen
sabed—¡pobre Granada!—, en su Granada ...

II

EL POETA Y LA MUERTE

Se le vió caminar solo con Ella,
sin miedo a su guadaña.
—Ya el sol en torre y torre; los martillos
en yunque—yunque y yunque de las fraguas.
Hablaba Federico,
requebrando a la muerte. Ella escuchaba.
"Porque ayer en mi verso, compañera,
sonaba el golpe de tus secas palmas,
y diste el hielo a mi cantar, y el filo
a mi tragedia de tu hoz de plata,
te cantaré la carne que no tienes,
los ojos que te faltan,
tus cabellos que el viento sacudía,
los rojos labios donde te besaban ...

THE CRIME WAS IN GRANADA

I
THE CRIME

He was seen walking, rifles at each side,
down the long street,
going out to the cold field,
still under the late stars of dawn.
Federico was slain
when the first light showed.
The firing squad
dared not look him in the face.
All shut their eyes;
they prayed: Not even God can save you!
Federico fell dead—
blood on his brow, lead in his heart—
The crime, remember, was in Granada,—
poor Granada!—in his Granada.

II
THE POET AND DEATH

Fearless of her sickle he was seen
walking alone with Her.
Now fell the sun on tower and tower; the hammers
on anvil—anvil and anvil of the forges.
Federico was speaking
flatteringly to Death. She listened.
"Because yesterday, comrade, in my verse,
the blow of your dry palms sounded,
and you gave ice to my singing, and to my tragedy
your silver sickle's edge,
I will sing you the flesh that you have not,
the eyes that you lack,
your hair that the wind was wont to shake,
the scarlet lips where they kissed you . . .

229

Hoy como ayer, gitana, muerte mía,
qué bien contigo a solas,
por estos aires de Granada, ¡mi Granada!"

III

Se le vió caminar...

Labrad, amigos,
de piedra y sueño, en el Alhambra,
un túmulo al poeta,
sobre una fuente donde llore el agua,
y eternamente diga:
el crimen fué en Granada, ¡en su Granada!

Today as yesterday, gypsy, my death,
how gladly I go with you alone
through these winds of Granada, my Granada!"

III

They were seen walking . . .
                              Friends, build
in the Alhambra, of stone and dreams,
the poet's tomb,
above a fountain where water weeps,
eternally saying,
the crime was in Granada, in his Granada!

H. E. F.

Notes

Entries not given in full are to be found in References (p. 235-242).

1 Baeza, Ricardo. *"Azorín" y la generación del 98.* In his *Comprensión de Dostoiewsky y otros ensayos.* Barcelona [ᶜ1935] p.185, *tr.*

2 Alonso, Dámaso. *Ensayos sobre poesía española.* Madrid [ᶜ1944] p.344, *tr.*

3 Jiménez, Juan Ramón. *Antonio Machado (1919).* In his *Españoles de tres mundos.* Buenos Aires [ᶜ1942]. p.74-75.

4 Dos Passos, John. *Rosinante to the road again.* New York [1922] p.208.

5 Gómez Alfaro. *Nuevo perfil.* p.3.

6 Del Arco. *Ricardo Calvo.* In *La vanguardia española.* Barcelona. October 26, 1958. p.29, *tr.*

7 Machado y Ruiz, Manuel. *La guerra literaria (1898-1914).* Madrid, 1913. p.27-28, *tr.*

8 García Blanco. *Cartas.* p.271, *tr.*

9 Ghiraldo, Alberto. *El archivo de Rubén Darío.* Santiago, Chile [1940] p.85, *tr.*

10 Darío, Rubén. *Opiniones.* Madrid [1918] p.74, *tr.*

11 Machado y Ruiz, Manuel. *Día por día de mi calendario.* Madrid, 1918. p.160, *tr.*

12 Baroja y Nessi, Pío. *Memorias.* Madrid, 1955. p.370, *tr.*

13 Machado y Ruiz, Antonio. *Páginas escogidas.* Madrid, 1917. p.15, *tr.*

14 Ford, Jeremiah Denis Matthias. *Old Spanish readings.* Boston, New York [1911] p.23, *tr.*

15 Machado y Ruiz, Antonio. *Obras.* México [1940]. p.620, *tr.*

16 Unamuno y Jugo, Miguel de. *Ensayos.* Madrid, 1917. v.5, p.31, *tr.*

17 Palau de Nemes, Graciela. *Vida y obra de Juan Ramón Jiménez.* Madrid [ᶜ1957] p.130, *tr.*

18 Ribbans. *La influencia de Verlaine.* p.184.

19 Machado y Ruiz, Antonio. *Reflexiones sobre la lírica; El libro* Colección *del poeta andaluz José Moreno Villa (1924).* In *Revista de occidente.* Madrid. 1925. año 3, no.24, p.368, *tr.*

20 *Ibid.* p.375, *tr.*

21 Cansinos Assens, Rafael. *La nueva literatura (1898-1900-1916)*. Madrid [19-?] v.2, p.250-251, *tr*.

22 *Ibid.* v.1, p.140; 139, *tr.*

23 Machado y Ruiz, Antonio. *Páginas escogidas*. Madrid, 1917. p.7, *tr.*

24 Diego, Gerardo. *Manuel Machado (1874-1947)*. In *Revista de Indias*. Madrid. July-December 1948. año 8 [i.e.9] nos.33-34, p.1167.

25 Brenan, Gerald. *South from Granada*. London [1957] p.266.

26 Machado y Ruiz, Antonio. *Obras*. México [1940] p.477, *tr.*

27 *Ibid.* p.787, *tr.*

28 Rosales, Luis. *Muerte y resurrección de Antonio Machado*. In *Cuadernos hispanoamericanos*. Madrid. 1949. nos. 11-12, p.435-479.

29 Cernuda. *Antonio Machado (1876-1939)*. p.114.

30 García Blanco. *Cartas*. p.106, *tr.*

31 *Ibid.* p.103-104, *tr.*

32 Landa. p.4, *tr.*

33 García Blanco. *Cartas*. p.113, *tr.*

34 Letter dated December 14, 1957 from Dr. José Gallego-Díaz, quoted with his courteous permission.

35 García Blanco. *Cartas*. p.272, *tr.*

36 Cernuda. *Antonio Machado (1876-1939)*. p.106, *tr.*

37 Machado y Ruiz, Antonio. *Obras*. México [1940] p.402, 601, *tr.*

38 Machado y Ruiz, Manuel. *La guerra literaria (1898-1914)*. Madrid, 1913. p.37.

39 Machado y Ruiz, Antonio. *Los complementarios*. p.39, *tr.*

40 Machado y Ruiz, Manuel. *Día por día de mi calendario*. Madrid, 1918. p.30.

41 Darío, Rubén. *Opiniones*. Madrid [1918] p.202, *tr.*

42 Segura Otaño, Enrique. *Antonio Machado y el poeta Monterrey; una visita inesperada*. In *Clavileño*. Madrid. March-April 1954. año 5, no.26, p.51-55.

43 Cassou. *Trois poètes*. p.94, *tr.*

44 Machado y Ruiz, Antonio. *Cuadernos de literatura. Baeza, 1915*, ed. by Enrique Casamayor. Bogotá, 1952.

45 Vivanco. *Retrato*. p.260-262.

46 *Ibid.* p.253-254, *tr.*

47 Machado y Ruiz, Antonio. *Los complementarios*. p.16, *tr.*

48 *Ibid.* p.[73]-77.

49 *Ibid.* p.63, *tr.*

233

50   Idem. *Obras*. México [1940] p.408, *tr.*

51   *Ibid.* p.602, *tr.*

52   Plá y Beltrán. p.235, *tr.*

53   Espina. p.56, *tr.*

54   Cano, José Luis. *Un amor de Machado: Guiomar*. In *Cuadernos del congreso por la libertad de la cultura*. Paris. 1959. no.36, p.41.

55   Fernández-Flores, Darío. *Memorias de un señorito*. Madrid [1956] p.267, *tr.*

56   Espina. p.83, *tr.*

57   Carpintero. *Historia*. p.320.

58   *Antonio Machado: obra inédita*. In *Revista hispánica moderna*. January-December 1949. año 15, nos.1-4, p.239, *tr.*

59   O'Connor, Frank. *The mirror in the roadway*. New York [c1956] p.225.

60   Machado y Ruiz, Antonio. *Obras*. México [1940] p.711-712, *tr.*

61   *Ibid.* p.557, *tr.*

62   *Ibid.* p.456, *tr.*

63   Idem. *Juan de Mairena*. Madrid, 1936. p.216, *tr.*

64   Idem. *Obras*. México [1940] p.472, *tr.*

65   *Ibid.* p.714, *tr.*

66   *Ibid.* p.446, *tr.*

67   Jiménez Martos, Luis. *Poema a las botas rotas de Antonio Machado, profesor de francés*. In Millán, Rafael, ed. *Antología de poesía española, 1954-1955*. Madrid, 1955.

68   Espina. p.112, *tr.*

69   Machado y Ruiz, Antonio. *Obras*. México [1940] p.466, *tr.*

70   *Ibid.* p.358, *tr.*

71   Idem. *Notas de actualidad*. In *Madrid*. Valencia. February 1937. no.1, p.10.

72   Ontañón, Eduardo de. *Muerte—en la arena—de Antonio Machado*. In his *Viaje y aventura de los escritores de España*. Mexico City [1942] p.95, *tr.*

73   Barga, Corpus. *Antonio Machado ante el destierro; detalles inéditos de su salida de España*. In *La Nación*. Lima. July 29, 1956. [n.p.]

74   Alvarez-Sierra, J. *La enfermedad y la muerte de Antonio Machado*. In *ABC*. Madrid. February 22, 1959. [n.p.]

References

Alberti, Rafael. *Imagen primera y sucesiva de Antonio Machado*. In his *Imagen primera de...Federico García Lorca, Juan Ramón Jiménez, etc.* Buenos Aires [c1945] p.[41]-59.

Alonso, Dámaso. *Fuente y jardín en la poesía de Machado*. In *Cuadernos hispanoamericanos*. Madrid, September-December 1949. nos.11-12, p.375-381.

————Poesías olvidadas de Antonio Machado. In his *Poetas españoles contemporáneos*. Madrid [c1952] p.[103]-159.

Alvarado, José. *Antonio Machado*. In *Taller*. México, 1939. no.3, p.23-[29].

Andrés Cobos, Pablo. *Recuerdos*. In *Indice de artes y letras*. Madrid, March 1958. año 12, no.111, p.7-8.

Aranguren, José Luis L. *Esperanza y desesperanza de Dios en la experiencia de la vida de Antonio Machado*. In *Cuadernos hispanoamericanos*. Madrid, September-December 1949. nos.11-12, p.383-397.

Arce, Margot. *Sobre "El viajero" de Antonio Machado*. In *Revista de la asociación de mujeres graduadas. [Hispania]* University of Puerto Rico, San Juan, 1939. v.1, p.[20]-25.

Aub, Max. *Antonio Machado*. In his *La poesía española contemporánea*. México, 1954. p.61-71.

————La seriedad de Antonio Machado: notas a su margen a los 17 años de su muerte. In *Cuadernos americanos*. México, March-April 1956. año 15, v.86, no.2, p.[211]-216.

Ayala, Francisco. *Antonio Machado: el poeta y la patria; ejemplos y pretextos*. In his *Histrionismo y representación*. Buenos Aires [1944] p.[163]-175.

Ayala, Juan Antonio. *La tierra de Alvargonzález. Estudio comparativo de dos textos de Antonio Machado*. In *Armas y letras; boletín...de la Universidad de Nuevo León*. Monterrey, Mexico, April-June 1958. año 1 [no.2] 2.época, p.57-75.

Barja, César. *Antonio Machado*. In his *Libros y autores contemporáneos*. Madrid [1935] p.[422]-438.

Beceiro, Carlos. *Antonio Machado y su visión paradójica de Castilla*. In *Celtiberia*. Soria, January-June 1958. año 8, v.8, no.15, p.[127]-142.

————El poema "A José María Palacio" de Antonio Machado. In *Insula*. Madrid, April 15, 1958. no.137, p.5.

————La tierra de Alvargonzález; un poema prosificado. In *Clavileño*. Madrid, September-October 1956. año 7, no.41, p.36-46.

Bergamín, José. *Antonio Machado*. In Machado y Ruiz, Antonio. *Obras*. México [1940] p.9-21.

————*Jardín en flor, y en sombra, y en silencio*...In *Hora de España*. Valencia, 1938. no.21, p.21-23.

Blasco Garzón, Manuel. *Gloria y pasión de Antonio Machado*. Buenos Aires [1942]

Bo, Carlo. *Observaciones sobre Antonio Machado*. In *Cuadernos hispano americanos*. Madrid, September-December 1949. nos.11-12, p.523-539.

Bousoño, Carlos. *El símbolo bisémico en la poesía de Antonio Machado; Tiempo futuro sobre tiempo presente: en Antonio Machado; Condensación temporal*. In his *Teoría de la expresión poética*...2.ed. Madrid [c1956] p.113-153, 155-158, 167-171.

Bula Piriz, Roberto. *Antonio Machado, 1875-1939*. [Montevideo] 1954.

C., E. [i.e. Enrique Casamayor?] *Un poema inédito de Antonio Machado*. In *Indice de artes y letras*. Madrid, March 1955. año 10, no.78, p.[1]

Cabral, Manuel del. *Hojeando a Machado*. In *Cuadernos hispanoamericanos*. Madrid, September-December 1949. nos.11-12, p.427-434.

Cano, José Luis. *Cartas de amor de Antonio Machado*. In *Insula*. Madrid, 1950. v.5, no.56.

————*Más sobre las cartas de amor de Antonio Machado; respuesta a un artículo de Jerónimo Mallo*. In *Correo literario*. Madrid, 1952. v.3, no.48.

————*Tres notas sobre Antonio Machado: 1. Antonio Machado, hombre y poeta en sueños; 2. Quimera y poesía (Bécquer y Machado); 3. La espina arrancada*. In his *De Machado a Bousoño; notas sobre poesía española contemporánea*. Madrid, 1955. p.13-44.

Cardenal de Iracheta, Manuel. *Crónica de Don Antonio y sus amigos en Segovia*. In *Cuadernos hispanoamericanos*. Madrid, September-December 1949. nos.11-12, p.301-306.

Carpintero, Heliodoro. *Boda de Antonio Machado*. In *ABC*. Madrid, February 16, 1957.

————*Historia y poesía de Antonio Machado; Soria, constante de su vida*. In *Celtiberia*. Soria, July-December 1951. año 1, v.1., no.2, p.[307]-355.

————*Unas páginas casi desconocidas de Antonio Machado*. In *Insula*. Madrid, August 15, 1955. año 10, no.116, p.3.

————*Soria, en la vida y en la obra de Antonio Machado*. In *Escorial*. Madrid, July 1943. v.12, no.33, p.111-127.

Casamayor, Enrique. *Antonio Machado, profesor de literatura*. In *Cuadernos hispanoamericanos*. Madrid, September-December 1949. nos.11-12, p.481-498.

————*Antonio Machado y sus inéditos "complementarios". (Un "cancionero" apócrifo con quince poetas de invención machadiana)*. In *Clavileño*. Madrid, May-June 1955. año 6, no.33, p.35-45.

Cassou, Jean. *Antonio Machado*. In *Hispania*. Paris, January-March 1920. p.[244]-248.

————*Trois poètes: Rilke, Milosz, Machado*. Paris [c1954] p.[85]-115.

Cejador y Frauca, Julio. *Antonio Machado y Ruiz*. In his *Historia de la lengua y literatura castellana*. Madrid, 1920. v.12, p.83-89.

Cernuda, Luis. *Antonio Machado (1876-1939)*. In his *Estudios sobre poesía española contemporánea*. Madrid-Bogotá [c1957] p.[105]-118.

————*Antonio Machado y la actual generación de poetas*. In *Bulletin of Spanish studies*. Liverpool, July 1940. v.17, no.67, p.139-143.

Chabás Martí, Juan. *Antonio Machado.* In his *Vuelo y estilo; estudios de literatura contemporánea.* Madrid [1934] v.1, p.61-[94].

Chacón y Calvo, José María. *El poeta de Soria (Antonio Machado).* In his *Ensayos sentimentales.* San José de Costa Rica, 1923. p.141-149.

Clavería, Carlos. *Notas sobre la poética de Antonio Machado.* In his *Cinco estudios de literatura española moderna.* Salamanca, 1945. p.[95]-118.

Conde, Carmen. *Cuando los poetas hablan a Dios.* In *Rueca.* México, 1943. v.2, no.8, p.40-49.

Corrales Egea, J. *Carta de París; el homenaje de los pintores a Antonio Machado.* In *Insula.* Madrid, March 15, 1955. año 10, no.111, p.5.

[Crispo Acosta, Osvaldo] *Antonio Machado y sus Soledades,* by Lauxar [pseud.]. In *Hispania.* Stanford University, California, May 1929. v.12, no.3, p.225-242.

Crow, John A. *The death of Antonio Machado.* In *The modern language forum.* Los Angeles, September 1939. v.24, no.3, p.133-140.

Darmangeat, Pierre. *Machado: poet of solitude.* In *Cronos.* Columbus, Ohio, 1948. v.2, no.4, p.[51]-63.

Diego, Gerardo. *"Tempo" lento en Antonio Machado.* In *Cuadernos hispanoamericanos.* Madrid, September-December 1949. nos.11-12, p.421-426.

Díez-Canedo, Enrique. *Antonio Machado, poeta japonés.* In *Repertorio americano.* San José de Costa Rica, June 11, 1927. p.351.

Dos Passos, John. *Antonio Machado: poet of Castile.* In his *Rosinante to the road again.* New York [c1922] p.140-158.

Edijimo [pseud.] *Nuestros compañeros: D. Antonio Machado y Ruiz.* In *Revista de segunda enseñanza.* [Madrid?] November 1926. año 4, no.26, p.358-360.

Espina, Concha. *De Antonio Machado a su grande y secreto amor.* Madrid [1950]

Espinoza, Enrique. *Conciencia poética de Antonio Machado.* In *Babel.* Santiago, Chile, 1949. v.12, p.47-64.

Estrella Gutiérrez, Fermín. *Antonio Machado, el poeta, el hombre.* In *Revista cubana.* Havana, January-December 1948. p.133-163.

Ferreres, Rafael. *Sobre la interpretación de un poema de Antonio Machado.* In *Cuadernos hispanoamericanos.* Madrid, July 1954. no.55, p.99-111.

Florit, Eugenio. *Antonio Machado.* In *Lyceum.* Havana, April-June 1939. v.4, no.14, p.3-14.

Frank, Waldo. *Death of Spain's poet: Antonio Machado.* In *The nation.* New York, April 15, 1939. p.[433]-436.

Gaos, Vicente. *Recuerdo de Antonio Machado; el recuerdo de los horas inolvidables.* In *El Español.* Madrid, January 6, 1945.

García Blanco, Manuel. *Cartas inéditas de Antonio Machado a Unamuno.* In *Revista hispánica moderna.* New York, 1956. año 22, p.[97]-114, [270]-285.

———*Un poema olvidado de Unamuno y una carta inédita de Antonio Machado.* In *Cultura universitaria.* Caracas, 1952. no.34, p.[59]-70.

García-Luengo, Eusebio. *Notas sobre la obra dramática de los Machado.* In *Cuadernos hispanoamericanos.* Madrid, September-December 1949. nos.11-12, p.667-676.

237

García-Viñó, Manuel. *El paisaje poético de Antonio Machado.* In *Archivo hispalense.* Sevilla, May-June 1956. 2.época, v.24, no.77, p.[259]-273.

Gicovate, Bernardo. *El testamento poético de Antonio Machado.* In The Modern language association of America. *Publications.* Boston, March, 1956, v.71, pt.1, no.1, p.42-50.

Giusti, Roberto F. *Antonio Machado; conferencia leída en el colegio el 12 de mayo de 1939.* In *Cursos y conferencias.* University of Buenos Aires, November 1939. año 8, v.15, no.8, p.[737]-763.

———*Antonio Machado: 'de "Soledades" a "Campos de Castilla."'* In *Nosotros.* Buenos Aires, May-June 1939. 2. época, año 4, nos.38-39, p.[5]-16.

Gómez Alfaro, Antonio. *Nuevo perfil humano de Antonio Machado (una entrevista con Don Ricardo Calvo).* In *Poesía española.* Madrid, May 1958. 2.época, no.70, p.1-5.

González, Rafael A. *Pensamiento filosófico de Antonio Machado.* In *La torre; revista general de la Universidad de Puerto Rico.* San Juan, April-June 1957. año 5, no.18, p.129-160.

Grant, Helen F. *Antonio Machado and 'La tierra de Alvargonzález'.* In *Atlante.* London, July 1954. v.2, no.3, p.[139]-158.

———*La tierra de Alvargonzález.* In *Celtiberia.* Soria, January-June 1953. año 2, v.3, no.5, p.[57]-81.

Grau, Mariano. *Antonio Machado en Segovia; conferencia dada en los cursos de verano de Segovia el 26 de julio de 1951.* In Cursos para extranjeros en Segovia. *Homenaje a Antonio Machado; conferencias.* Segovia, 1952, p.19-28.

Guerra, Manuel H. *Antonio Machado, autor teatral.* In *The modern language journal.* Boston, October 1951. v.35, no.6, p.447-454.

Guerrero Ruiz, Juan, and Casamayor, Enrique. *Bibliografía de Antonio Machado.* In *Cuadernos hispanoamericanos.* Madrid, September-December 1949. nos.11-12, p.703-711.

Guillén, Claudio. *Estilística del silencio (en torno a un poema de Antonio Machado).* In *Revista hispánica moderna.* New York, 1957. v.23, nos.3-4, p.[260]-291.

Gullón, Ricardo. *Lenguaje, humanismo y tiempo en Antonio Machado.* In *Cuadernos hispanoamericanos.* Madrid, September-December 1949. nos.11-12, p.567-581.

———*Las secretas galerías de Antonio Machado.* [Madrid, c1958]

———*Simbolismo en la poesía de Antonio Machado.* In *Clavileño.* Madrid, July-August, 1953. año 4, p.44-50.

———*Unidad en la obra de Antonio Machado.* In *Insula.* Madrid, April 15, 1949. año 4, no.40, p.[1].

Heliodoro Valle, Rafael. *Antonio Machado: bibliografía.* In *Revista hispánica moderna.* New York, January-December 1949. año 15, nos.1-4, p.[81]-98.

Hennick, Janet Meyers. *El paisaje de Soria y la visión de España en Antonio Machado.* In *Celtiberia.* Soria, 1954. v.5, p.199-228.

Izquierdo, Julián. *Antonio Machado, valor universal de España.* In *Indice de artes y letras.* Madrid, September 30, 1953. año 8, no.67, p.5-6.

Jiménez, Juan Ramón. *Antonio Machado,* In *Insula.* Madrid, November 15, 1958. año 12, no.144, p.[1]-2.

————*Tres poetas en Antonio Machado.* In *Revista de la asociación patriótica española.* Buenos Aires, 1945. v.18, no.207.

Kercheville, Francis Monroe. *A study of tendencies in modern and contemporary Spanish poetry from the modernist movement to the present time.* In The University of New Mexico. *Bulletin.* Albuquerque, December 15, 1933. v.4, no.2, p.37-43.

Laín Entralgo, Pedro. *La memoria y la esperanza: San Agustín, San Juan de la Cruz, Antonio Machado, Miguel de Unamuno; discurso [en la R. Academia española].* Madrid, 1954. p.75-97.

Landa, Rubén. *Mis recuerdos de Antonio Machado.* In *Suplemento de El nacional.* San Juan, February 20, 1955. p.4, 10.

Lapesa Melgar, Rafael. *Bécquer, Rosalía y Machado.* In *Insula.* Madrid, April 30, 1954. año 9, nos.100-101, p.6.

Lázaro Carreter, Fernando. *Glosa a un poema de Antonio Machado.* In *Insula.* Madrid, November 15, 1958. no.119, p.11, 19.

————*Juan Ramón, A. Machado y García Lorca; aproximaciones.* In *Insula.* Madrid, July-August 1957. año 12, nos.128-129, p.[1], 5, 21.

Lefebvre, Alfredo. *Notas sobre la poesía de Antonio Machado.* In *Cuadernos hispanoamericanos.* Madrid, September-December 1949. nos.11-12, p.323-332.

Levi, Ezio. *Antonio Machado.* In *Hispania.* Stanford University, California, 1928. v.11, p.471-476.

López-Morillas, Juan. *Antonio Machado's temporal interpretation of poetry.* In *The journal of aesthetics and art criticism.* [Baltimore] December 1947. v.6, no.2, p.161-171.

Machado y Ruiz, Antonio. *Los complementarios y otras prosas póstumas,* ed. by Guillermo de Torre. Buenos Aires [c1957]

————*Prólogo; Nota biográfica; Soledades.* In his *Páginas escogidas.* Madrid, 1917. p.7-10; 11; 15-16.

Machado y Ruiz, Joaquín. *Relámpagos del recuerdo.* In *Atenea.* Universidad de Concepción, Chile, 1951. no.101, p.[377]-384.

Machado y Ruiz, José. *Ultimas soledades del poeta Antonio Machado (recuerdos de su hermano José).* [Santiago de Chile? 195-?]

Mallo, Jerónimo. *La idealogía religiosa y política del poeta Antonio Machado.* In *Symposium.* Syracuse, New York, 1955. v.9, no.2, p.339-347.

————*Sobre el "grande y secreto amor" de Antonio Machado.* In *Cuadernos americanos.* México, 1952. v.11, no.1, p.[214]-236.

Marañón y Posadillo, Gregorio. *Prólogo.* In Pérez Ferrero, Miguel. *Vida.* p.[13]-25.

Marías, Julián. *Antonio Machado y su interpretación poética de las cosas.* In *Cuadernos hispanoamericanos.* Madrid, September-December 1949. nos.11-12, p.307-321.

————*Machado y Heidegger.* In *Suplemento de Insula.* Madrid, October 15, 1953. año 8, no.94, p.[1]-2.

Marquerie, Alfredo. *El teatro de Machado; extracto de la conferencia dada en los cursos de verano, el 28 de julio de 1951.* In Cursos para extranjeros en Segovia. *Homenaje a Antonio Machado; conferencias.* Segovia, 1952. p.43-47.

Martínez Sierra, Gregorio. *El madrigal nuevo*. In *Renacimiento*. Madrid, May 1907. no.3, p.[349]-381.

Mejía Sánchez, Ernesto. *Centroamerica y los Machado*. In *Revista de Guatemala*. Guatemala City, 1951. v.3, no.3, p.185-190.

Mélich Orsini, José. *En torno al pensamiento de Antonio Machado*. In *Revista nacional de cultura*. Caracas, 1946. v.7, no.58, p.67-87.

Milazzo, Elena. *Antonio Machado*. Lugano, 1958.

Molina, A. R. *Ver y mirar en la obra poética de Antonio Machado*. In *Papeles de Son Armadans*. Madrid, Palma de Mallorca, December 1956. año 1, v.3, no.9, p.241-264.

Montero Alonso, José. *Por los caminos de España; la cueva del anacoreta y los versos de Antonio Machado*. In *ABC*. Madrid, May 19, 1955.

Montserrat, Santiago. *Antonio Machado, poeta y filósofo*. Buenos Aires [c1943].

Moreno de Páramo, Ismael. *Antonio Machado, en mi niñez*. In *Indice de artes y letras*. Madrid. May 30, 1953. año 8, no.63, p.20.

—————*Antonio Machado y aquel niño que yo fui*. In *Correo literario*. Madrid, February 15, 1954. año 5, no.90, p.[1], 14.

Moreno Villa, José. *Las cinco palabras de Antonio Machado*. In his *Leyendo a San Juan de la Cruz*. México [1946] p.85-99.

Mostaza, Bartolomé. *El paisaje en la poesía de Antonio Machado*. In *Cuadernos hispanoamericanos*. Madrid, September-December 1949. nos.11-12, p.623-641.

Muñoz Alonso, Adolfo. *Sueño y razón en la poesía de Antonio Machado*. In *Cuadernos hispanoamericanos*. Madrid. September-December 1949, nos.11-12, p.643-651.

Nogales, María Antonia. *Antonio Machado y el barroco literario*. In *Archivum; revista de la Facultad de filosofía y letras, Universidad de Oviedo*. Oviedo, January-April 1955. v.5, fasc.1, p.148-157.

Nora, Eugenio de. *Machado ante el futuro de la poesía lírica*. In *Cuadernos hispanoamericanos*. Madrid, September-December 1949. nos.11-12, p.583-592.

Oliver Belmás, Antonio. *Antonio Machado: ensayo crítico sobre su tiempo y su poesía*. [Bilbao, 1948?]

Onís y Sánchez, Federico de. *Antonio Machado, poeta predilecto*. In Hispanic institute in the United States. *Antonio Machado (1875-1939)...*New York, 1951. p.[7]-10.

Ortega y Gasset, José, *Los versos de Antonio Machado*. In his *Personas, obras, cosas...*2.ed. Madrid, 1916. p.[327]-334.

Pasqua, Juan. *Antonio Machado en Baeza*. In *ABC*. Madrid, April 17, 1959.

Peers, Edgar Allison. *Antonio Machado. (The Taylorian lecture, 1939)*. Oxford, 1940.

Pemán, José María. *El tema del limonero y la fuente en Antonio Machado. (Discurso pronunciado en Sevilla el 27 de abril de 1952, en el Palacio de las Dueñas, con ocasión del descubrimiento de una lápida en memoria de Antonio Machado)*. In R. Academia española, Madrid. *Boletín*. May-August 1952. año 41, v.32, cuad. 136, p.[171]-191.

Perez Ferrero, Miguel. *Vida de Antonio Machado y Manuel*. [Madrid, 1947]

Phillips, Allen W. *"La tierra de Alvargonzález"; verso y prosa*. In *Nueva revista de filología hispánica*. México, April-June 1955. año 9, no.2, p.[129]-148.

Plá y Beltrán, Pascual. *Mi entrevista con Antonio Machado*. In *Cuadernos americanos*. México, January-February 1954. v.73, no.1, p.[233]-238.

Posada, José. *Leonor*. In *Cuadernos hispanoamericanos*. Madrid, September-December 1949. nos.11-12, p.415-417.

Pradal-Rodríguez, Gabriel. *Antonio Machado: vida y obras*. In *Revista hispánica moderna*. New York, January-December 1949. año 15, nos. 1-4, p.[1]-80.

Predmore, Richard Lionel. *El tiempo en la poesía de Antonio Machado*. In The Modern language association of America. *Publications*. Boston, June 1948. v.63, no.2, pt.1, p.696-711.

———*La visión de Castilla en la obra de Antonio Machado*. In *Hispania*. Washington, November 1946. v.29, no.4, p.500-506.

Quintanilla, Mariano. *El pensamiento de Antonio Machado; extracto de la conferencia dada en los cursos de verano de Segovia el 27 de julio de 1951*. In Cursos para extranjeros en Segovia. *Homenaje a Antonio Machado; conferencias*. Segovia, 1952. p.29-42.

R.C.P. *La máquina de trovar electrónica*. In *Cuadernos hispanoamericanos*. Madrid. August 1953. no.44, p.265-266.

Regalado, Antonio. *Antonio Machado, poeta español de la generación del 98*. In *Universidad de La Habana*. Havana, 1944. v.9, no.52, p.151-180.

Revilla, Angel. *La vida y la obra de Antonio Machado; conferencia dada en los cursos de verano de Segovia el 25 de julio de 1951*. In Cursos para extranjeros en Segovia. *Homenaje a Antonio Machado; conferencias*. Segovia, 1952. p.5-17.

Ribbans, Geoffrey W. *La influencia de Verlaine en Antonio Machado (Con nuevos datos sobre la primera época del poeta)*. In *Cuadernos hispanoamericanos*. Madrid, July-August 1957. nos.91-92, p.180-201.

———*Un texto desconocido de Antonio Machado*. In *Bulletin hispanique*. Bordeaux, October-December 1957. v.59, no.4, p.[415]-417.

———*Unamuno and Antonio Machado*. In *Bulletin of hispanic studies*. Liverpool, January 1957. v.34, no.1, p.10-28.

Rodríguez, Hernán. *Conflicto de vida y muerte en la obra de Antonio Machado*. In *Minerva*. Buenos Aires, 1944. v.1, no.1, p.[55]-59.

Salinas, Pedro. *Antonio Machado*. In his *Literatura española, siglo xx*. México [1941] p.213-223.

Sánchez Barbudo, Antonio. *El pensamiento de "Abel Martín" y "Juan de Mairena" y su relación con la poesía de Antonio Machado*. In *Hispanic review*. Philadelphia, 1954. v.22, p.32-74, 109-165.

Sánchez Vázquez, Adolfo. *Humanismo y visión de España en Antonio Machado*. In *Filosofía y letras*. México, 1952. v.24, p.61-77.

Santullano, Luis A. *Semblanza de Antonio Machado*. In Machado y Ruiz, José. *Ultimas soledades del poeta Antonio Machado (recuerdos de su hermano José)*. [Santiago de Chile? 195-?]

Serrano Plaja, Arturo. *Antonio Machado*. Buenos Aires [1944]

Serrano Poncela, Segundo. *Antonio Machado; su mundo y su obra*. Buenos Aires [c1954]

241

Sloman, Albert E. *La fecha de un poema de A. Machado.* In *Clavileño.* Madrid, May-June 1954. año 5, no.27, p.56.

Sobejano Mainz, Gonzalo. *Notas tradicionales en la lírica de Antonio Machado.* In *Romanische forschungen.* Frankfort, 1954. v.66, p.[112]-151.

Torre, Guillermo de. *Antonio Machado y sus poetas apócrifos.* In *Insula.* Madrid, May 15, 1957. año 12, no.126, p.[1]-2.

——*Identidad y desdoblamientos de Antonio Machado.* In *Cuadernos del congreso por la libertad de la cultura.* Paris, 1959. no.36, p.33-38.

——*Poesía y ejemplo de Antonio Machado.* In his *Tríptico del sacrificio. Unamuno, García Lorca, Machado.* Buenos Aires [1948] p.[89]-113.

Trend, John Brande. *Antonio Machado; with an appendix of verse and prose not included in the collected editions.* Oxford, 1953.

——*The brothers Machado.* In his *Alfonso the sage and other Spanish essays.* Boston, New York, 1926. p.[135]-146.

Tudela, José. *Soria y Machado.* In *Celtiberia.* Soria, 1953. p.275-279.

Tudela, Ricardo. *Juan de Mairena o la indagación de lo hispánico.* In *Ateneo.* San Salvador, 1937. v.39, no.146, p.[240]-256.

Vaccaro, Héctor. *El atisbo existencialista en Antonio Machado.* In *Revista hispánica moderna.* New York, July-October 1948. año 14, nos.3-4, p.[272]-276.

Valente, J. A. *Carta de Antonio Machado; "modernismo" y "98".* In *Indice de artes y letras.* Madrid, April-May 1954. año 9, nos.74-75, p.22-23.

Valverde, José María. *Evolución del sentido espiritual de la obra de Antonio Machado.* In *Cuadernos hispanoamericanos.* Madrid, September-December 1949. nos.11-12, p.399-414.

——*Sobre Antonio Machado.* In *Arbor.* Madrid, December 1948. v.11, no.36, p.560-564.

Vega Benayas, Carlos de la. *¿Poesía o filosofía? (Antonio Machado y "el otro").* In *Suplemento de Insula.* Madrid, October 15, 1953. v.8, no.94, p.2.

Vilariño, Idea. *Grupos simétricos en la poesía de Antonio Machado.* In *Número.* Montevideo, 1951. v.3, nos.15-17, p.[348]-355.

Villa Pastur, J. *Juan Ramón Jiménez ante la poesía de Miguel de Unamuno y Antonio Machado.* In *Archivum; revista de la Facultad de filosofía y letras, Universidad de Oviedo.* Oviedo, January-April 1955. v.5, fasc.1, p.136-147.

Vivanco, Luis Felipe. *Comentario a unos pocos poemas de Antonio Machado.* In *Cuadernos hispanoamericanos.* Madrid, September-December 1949. nos.11-12, p.564-565.

——*Retrato en el tiempo, un poema inédito de Antonio Machado.* In *Papeles de Son Armadans.* Madrid—Palma de Mallorca, September 1956. año 1, v.2, no.6, p.249-268.

Zubiría, Ramón de. *La poesía de Antonio Machado.* Madrid, 1955.

Index of Persons

Index of Poems

Issued in this Format

(Monographs, based on the museum and library collections, dealing with the arts and literature of Spain and showing their relation to those of other countries)

LUIS DE MORALES AND LEONARDESQUE INFLUENCES IN SPAIN
by Elizabeth du Gué Trapier

MUDEJAR ORNAMENT IN MANUSCRIPTS
by Frances Spalding

THE BOOK CALLED CELESTINA IN THE LIBRARY
OF THE HISPANIC SOCIETY OF AMERICA
by Clara Louisa Penney

GOYA: A STUDY OF HIS PORTRAITS 1797-99
by Elizabeth du Gué Trapier

CAPODIMONTE AND BUEN RETIRO PORCELAINS:
PERIOD OF CHARLES III
by Alice Wilson Frothingham

VALDÉS LEAL: BAROQUE CONCEPT OF DEATH AND SUFFERING
IN HIS PAINTINGS
by Elizabeth du Gué Trapier

POMPEO LEONI: WORK IN MARBLE AND ALABASTER
IN RELATION TO SPANISH SCULPTURE
by Beatrice Gilman Proske

BARCELONA GLASS IN VENETIAN STYLE
by Alice Wilson Frothingham

COSTUMES PAINTED BY SOROLLA IN HIS PROVINCES OF SPAIN
by Ruth Matilda Anderson

EL GRECO: EARLY YEARS AT TOLEDO, 1576-1586
by Elizabeth du Gué Trapier

———————

Printed by PETROCELLI PRESS, New York